10 Steps to Reducing Your Child's
Anxiety on the Autism Spectrum

by the same authors

Exploring Depression, and Beating the Blues
A CBT Self-Help Guide to Understanding and Coping with
Depression In Asperger's Syndrome [ASD-Level 1]
Tony Attwood and Michelle Garnett
ISBN 978 1 84905 502 4
eISBN 978 0 85700 907 4

**CBT to Help Young People with Asperger's Syndrome (Autism
Spectrum Disorder) to Understand and Express Affection**
A Manual for Professionals
Tony Attwood and Michelle Garnett
ISBN 978 1 84905 412 6
eISBN 978 0 85700 801 5

**From Like to Love for Young People with Asperger's
Syndrome (Autism Spectrum Disorder)**
Learning How to Express and Enjoy Affection with Family and Friends
Tony Attwood and Michelle Garnett
ISBN 978 1 84905 436 2
eISBN 978 0 85700 777 3

10 Steps to Reducing Your Child's Anxiety on the Autism Spectrum

The CBT-Based 'Fun with Feelings' Parent Manual

Michelle Garnett, Tony Attwood, Louise Ford,
Stefanie Runham and Julia Cook

Jessica Kingsley Publishers
London and Philadelphia

First published in 2020
by Jessica Kingsley Publishers
73 Collier Street
London N1 9BE, UK
and
400 Market Street, Suite 400
Philadelphia, PA 19106, USA

www.jkp.com

Library of Congress Cataloging in Publication Data
A CIP catalog record for this book is available from the Library of Congress

British Library Cataloguing in Publication Data
A CIP catalogue record for this book is available from the British Library

ISBN 978 1 78775 325 9
eISBN 978 1 78775 326 6

Printed and bound in Great Britain

Contents

Introduction and Overview of How to Use *Fun with Feelings* to Decrease Your Child's Anxiety

Why Young Children with ASD Need a Programme to Assist with Recognizing and Regulating their Emotions

The ability to recognize emotions and to regulate one's own feelings are key milestones that emerge from early childhood and develop through to adulthood. These fundamental skills provide the backbone to self-regulation, social understanding and positive relationships throughout the lifespan. Unfortunately, individuals with an autism spectrum disorder (ASD) often have significant difficulties with the identification and management of emotions, and this is particularly evident from early childhood.

> Throughout this book the authors have chosen to use the term ASD to describe an autism spectrum condition, including autism, Asperger's syndrome and other terms used to describe a subtype of autism.

Difficulties with the Identification, Expression and Understanding of Emotions

Young children with ASD have significant difficulties with the identification, expression and understanding of emotions. Typically developing children at 4–6 years of age can demonstrate basic emotions such as happiness, sadness, anger and fear on their faces when asked, as well as other more complex emotions, and additionally are able to identify a wide range of emotions within themselves and others. On the other hand, children with ASD often have trouble with intuitively manipulating their faces to the chosen emotion, perhaps only capturing one element of the emotion on their face. Some younger children with ASD may express their emotions through stereo-typical behaviours such as hand flapping when they are happy, or through other non-verbal behaviours such as stomping their feet, walking away and pushing. Additionally, young children with ASD find it difficult to name the emotion they are experiencing, and phrases used may be 'borrowed' from parents without a full understanding of their meaning.

Due to key difficulties with emotional recognition and understanding, young children with ASD also tend to overlook obvious signs of emotions from their parents and teachers. For example, they may fail to pick up anger in their parent or teacher through simply observing their folded arms or frown, or hearing their tone of voice. Emotional thinking, which connects events or actions to consequent feelings, is also difficult for children with ASD, whereas this is a skill that comes naturally to their peers. Consequently, young children with ASD struggle with cause and effect in relation to both their own and others' feelings.

Difficulties with Emotion Regulation and Anxiety

Young children with ASD can also have significant difficulties with regulating or managing their own emotions. Although many children and adults feel anxious, angry or stressed at times, young children with ASD are more vul-nerable to experiencing these emotions for longer periods of time and with greater intensity. In fact, research indicates that 75% of young ASD children experience greater levels of emotional reactivity than typically developing children of a similar age (Russell and Sofronoff, 2005). It is therefore not uncommon to see young children with ASD, who have little understanding about what they are feeling and little awareness of their increasing stress, being unable to stay calm in the seemingly unpredictable world around them. Being interrupted in the middle of their favourite cartoon or peers not play-ing by their rules may result in rapid and intense displays of anger. Similarly, experiences such as a change in the car route to preschool, interaction with peers, anticipation of a painful sensory experience and the presence of a relief teacher may all be sources of anxiety for these young children. At such times, the child will respond in one of two ways: they will either avoid the stimulus and retreat (flight) or tantrum and become aggressive (fight).

Young children with ASD are more prone to experiencing anxiety symptoms than their typically developing peers. In fact, research indicates that approximately 33% of young children with a high-functioning ASD have a co-occurring clinical anxiety disorder and up to 60% experience high levels of anxiety (Mayes *et al.*, 2011). In addition, their experience with increased anxiety is more severe than for typically developing children, and this anxiety increases the core deficits of ASD (Mayes *et al.*, 2011). Unfortunately, research also indicates that, without intervention, young children with ASD continue to have high rates of anxiety, and in fact the figure appears to increase into adolescence and adulthood. Therefore, it is important to engage young children with ASD in effective early intervention for anxiety and emotion regulation difficulties for skills acquisition and best outcomes as they develop.

Intense emotions, including anger and anxiety, experienced on a regular basis, leave the child, and often his parents, emotionally and physically exhausted. Engaging in frequent 'meltdowns' can result in the child with ASD being isolated from his peers, who may be frightened of his behaviour. The avoidance that often results from anxiety in the long term can also mean that the child has less opportunity to develop academic, emotional and social skills. For example, in relation to social anxiety, when the child retreats into a special interest or solitude instead of playing with a peer, there are fewer occasions for him to develop the skills of cooperation, flexibility, reciprocity, resiliency and friendship building. It is therefore not surprising that greater severity of social anxiety has been linked with lower assertive social skills (e.g. initiating conversations) and responsible social skills (e.g. asking permission to use people's belongings) for children and adolescents with ASD. In addition, for children with ASD, anxiety has been associated with increased family stress and conflict, school refusal, academic problems, increased negative automatic thoughts, feelings of loneliness, and depression, increased externalizing problem behaviour and decreased quality of life (Attwood, 2006; Cook, Donovan and Garnett, 2017; Mayes *et al.*, 2011; Plows, 2013). Consequently, treatments for managing anxiety specifically in children with ASD have been designed and evaluated.

Cognitive Behaviour Therapy

Cognitive behaviour therapy (CBT) is considered a 'gold standard' for the treatment of various psychological conditions across the lifespan including depression and anxiety. CBT has successfully been implemented with typically developing young children who experience clinically significant anxiety. Modified versions of CBT that include ASD adaptations have been successfully implemented with adolescents and adults with ASD with anxiety and mood disorders. Although there has been limited research focused specifically on the implementation of modified CBT for young children with ASD and emotion regulation difficulties, the limited studies that have been conducted show very promising results.

The *Fun with Feelings* programme was originally based on the *Exploring Anxiety* and *Exploring Anger* programmes developed by Tony Attwood (2004). These two programmes were designed for children with ASD from 8 to 12 years and have been evaluated by five independent research studies (Clarke, Hill and Charman, 2017; Luxford, Hadwin and Kovshoff, 2017; McConachie *et al.*, 2014; Sofronoff, Attwood and Hinton, 2005; Sofronoff *et al.*, 2007). Thus, the components of the *Fun with Feelings* programme are confirmed as being effective for children with ASD.

Additionally, the *Fun with Feelings* programme has been evaluated in two scientific research studies with younger children. The first study evaluated the effectiveness of the *Fun with Feelings* programme for improving emotion management difficulties in children with ASD aged 4–6 years of age (Plows, 2013). Children completed the *Fun with Feelings* activities in eight one-hour group sessions while their parents completed the parent activities in eight concurrent half-hour group sessions. After the programme, children showed improvements in both awareness of their emotions and their ability to manage their anxiety and anger. The second study evaluated the effectiveness of the *Fun with Feelings* programme when the programme is delivered by parents to their 4–6-year-old children, within the home. Parents attended ten 90-minute group sessions, in which they were taught the skills and strategies that are described in this book. They then completed the child activities with their children at home during the week between sessions (Cook *et al.*, 2017). Results showed reduction in the children's anxiety as a result of the programme, at a three-month follow-up after the programme had finished.

Aims of *Fun with Feelings*

The key aims of this programme are to provide knowledge to parents of young children with ASD to better understand their child's emotional skill set and empower them to have the confidence and competence to implement interventions that provide the stepping stones to support their child's improvement in these foundational identification and regulation skills – specifically:

- knowledge and identification of the basic emotions of happiness, sadness, relaxation, anxiety, anger and love within themselves and others
- use of language, especially speech, for emotional identification and recognizing intensity of emotions
- knowledge and use of relaxation and general emotion regulation skills with adult prompting.

At the end of the programme, we are *not* expecting the child to be proficient in each of these skills sets. This would not be a realistic expectation. Rather, this programme aims to support further growth in these areas for young children with ASD, which in turn provides a key foundational basis for more advanced social and emotional skills as they mature.

About *Fun with Feelings*

Fun with Feelings was developed by clinical psychologists at Minds & Hearts as a group cognitive behavioural therapy programme for parents and children aged 4–6 years to increase capacity within the child on the autism spectrum, and the family, to manage anxiety. However, we know that not all families can access a clinical psychologist with specialist knowledge and skills in autism. We set out to reinvent the programme as one that can be delivered by the parent at home. Equally, a clinical psychologist or other allied health professional may utilize this programme within therapy sessions with the parent. There are ten stages to *Fun with Feelings*, and these are paced to be implemented at the rate of approximately one stage per week, although there are no hard rules about this.

The aim of the initial four stages is to prepare the parent to implement the programme with their child. These stages contain a lot of valuable information to help the parent understand their child better, both his anxiety and ASD. The final six stages utilize this new understanding to help the parent implement *Fun with Feelings* with their child, using six activity booklets. Through their combined decades of clinical experience, the authors have discovered that the best outcomes for children with anxiety and ASD are the result of targeted interventions that are informed by a deep understanding of the child and involve parents and teachers.

> For ease of communication, the authors will refer to a child as he or she randomly throughout the book rather than use he/she. The authors will refer to parents throughout the book to refer to the primary carers of the child.

Each of the ten stages of *Fun with Feelings* contains information and activities to assist parents to better understand their child, her ASD and her anxiety. The knowledge and strategies within *Fun with Feelings* were derived from current research and decades of clinical experience working with children who have ASD and anxiety. We have designed *Fun with Feelings* with a deep understanding of the best ways to learn and implement new skills and ideas, incorporating self-monitoring tasks, opportunities for setting clear goals, making realistic plans, staging learning in easy-to-manage steps and using reflection to consolidate learning.

Goals and Planning
At the end of each stage of the *Fun with Feelings* programme there is the opportunity to create a Weekly Plan. The Weekly Plan gives the parent the opportunity to practise the skills and strategies learned through the reading and writing activities within each step. We include within the Stage 1 Weekly Plan a goal-setting tool to ensure that the family benefits as much as possible from *Fun with Feelings*. The Weekly Plan allows a fresh start to each week with a clear sense of the changes to make to support the child. You can be reassured that we include the strategies that we have found to have the most chance of working with children with ASD and have used these many times over in our own clinic.

Reflection
At the beginning of each stage of *Fun with Feelings*, parents will be asked to stop and reflect on how they implemented *Fun with Feelings* at home. We highly recommend that parents take the time to pause and reflect on what they did differently at the beginning of each new stage. Reflection increases

awareness of new insights and ensures that the new learning is integrated as a part of a reliable and easy-to-access knowledge base.

Frequently Asked Questions (FAQs)
There is a section at the end of each stage describing commonly found difficulties with the tasks of the Weekly Plan and suggestions for managing these challenges.

Understanding Anxiety in ASD

Overview of Stage 1

The aim of Stage 1 is to help you understand both your child's ASD and their anxiety. Understanding both is the key to assisting your child to cope with their challenges and build on their strengths.

During Stage 1 you will learn:

- ✓ What is ASD?
- ✓ What is anxiety?
- ✓ When do young children with ASD become anxious?
- ✓ What does anxiety look like in young children with ASD?
- ✓ What is a meltdown?
- ✓ What is the difference between meltdowns and tantrums?
- ✓ Goals for the programme.
- ✓ The Weekly Plan.

You will need:

- ✓ This book.

What is Autism Spectrum Disorder (ASD)?

There are so many words out there for ASD, including autism, high-functioning autism, Asperger's disorder and PDD-NOS, just for a start. In this book we are going to use the term ASD. ASD is a term to describe some unique aspects to the way a person's brain works. It is unfortunate that the term ASD has the word 'disorder' in it – as one little boy with ASD said, 'But my brain is very ordered!' We would prefer the 'D' in ASD to refer to 'difference'. Perhaps when you read ASD, you can think autism spectrum *difference*!

So what are the differences? Essentially, the person with ASD has a brain that does not innately or intuitively understand how to socialize with other people. Knowing how to socialize means knowing things like how to read a face, use body language, start a conversation, knowing why we use greetings and people's names, and knowing how to infer what people are thinking and expecting. There are degrees to this difference that range from having no idea about socializing, what it is and how to do it, all the way to being able to manage socializing reasonably well, by using other areas of the brain. In addition to having these social difficulties, the person with ASD has difficulties with processing the information coming to the brain through the senses and/or shows rigidity and repetition in their behaviour. In other words, they do not cope well with change or transitions and they tend to like to do things the same way over and over.

The degree to which a person experiences ASD is currently denoted as being Level 1, 2 or 3, based on how much support is needed. The levels of support are described separately for the two key components of ASD: social difficulty and rigidity/repetitive behaviours (RRBs). Level 1 is assigned when comparatively less support is required, moving up to Level 3 to indicate that considerable support is required. The levels may change over time depending on the person's stressors, social support and coping strategies.

In most cases, ASD is known to be genetically transmitted – that is, it is passed on via genes through families. Certain genetic conditions are known to cause ASD, such as fragile X syndrome. There are other pathways to ASD – for example, ASD is associated with having older parents, adverse obstetric events and certain medical conditions (e.g. tuberous sclerosis).

As our awareness and understanding of the subtle presentations of ASD develop, more and more individuals are being diagnosed with the condition. Indeed, current research suggests that as many as 1 in 59 people now have an ASD diagnosis (Baio *et al.*, 2018). Similarly, as our awareness and understanding of the way ASD manifests in girls, more and more girls are being diagnosed with ASD. Although ASD is known to be more prevalent in boys, our current estimate of the gender ratio is 1 girl for every 2 boys (Rutherford *et al.*, 2016), whereas the previous estimate was 1:4 (APA, 2013).

It is rare to have pure ASD; it is a brain difference that tends to co-occur with other brain differences. Intellectual disability, expressive language disorder, attention deficit hyperactivity disorder and specific learning disabilities (e.g. dyslexia) all commonly co-occur with ASD. Also, the genes for mood disorders (e.g. depression) are common in families that have the genes for ASD. Therefore, it is common for people with ASD to also experience anxiety and/or depression, in part because of genetic transmission.

It is important to keep in mind that ASD in not an illness or a disease, and therefore does not need a cure or treatment (although some of the co-occurring conditions, such as anxiety, may need treatment). ASD is a brain difference, and, clearly, difference can make life more challenging. However, it is equally important to recognize the gifts and strengths that are a part of the profile of ASD and to know that many people with ASD become active members of society with successful careers, fulfilling relationships and much-loved families.

The main problem for people with ASD is often not having ASD but the ignorance and misunderstanding that is still so prevalent in our society about ASD. Understanding ASD and how the condition relates to your child is a crucial way that you can support your child and be her voice in situations where other people need this understanding.

Every child with ASD has a unique personality and distinct likes, dislikes, gifts, strengths and difficulties. However, young children with ASD display similar strengths and challenges.

Activity: My Child's Strengths and Challenges

Below are descriptions of some strengths and challenges common in ASD. Read through each of the descriptions and note down any of your child's strengths and difficulties.

Perspective Taking (Theory of Mind)

- ☐ Children with ASD are generally remarkably honest.
- ☐ They can be extremely 'in tune' with, and sensitive to, other people's anxiety or agitation, feeling the emotion as if it were their own. Negative emotions seem to be 'contagious' for children with ASD.
- ☐ They may have difficulty understanding that other people have

opinions, beliefs and feelings that are different from their own. For example, they can find it very difficult to believe that their friends would like anything that they themselves do not like.

☐ They may expect others to have the same level of knowledge about an event they have experienced, even when these others were not present when this event occurred.

Notes

Social Interactions

☐ Children with ASD can be very caring and compassionate in friendships. Often these qualities do not emerge until later in childhood.

☐ They may or may not be interested in the social activities of their peers or in making friends.

☐ They may be found on the periphery of games/activities or playing alone.

☐ They may seek predictability and control in social interactions and struggle when others do not follow their rules or change their rules.

☐ They may experience difficulties with sharing, collaboration, reciprocity and spontaneity, and thus may be at the centre of conflict in the playground.

☐ They may have difficulty incorporating information they know about someone else into their way of interacting with that person. For example, they may know that other children do not care about bathrooms, but they continue to start conversations with other children about bathrooms.

Notes

Communication

- ☐ Children with ASD display a wide range of communication abilities.
- ☐ Their use of vocabulary, syntax and grammar may be excellent and somewhat 'adult like'.
- ☐ They may have difficulty engaging in conversation.
- ☐ They may make literal interpretations of phrases such as 'It's raining cats and dogs'.
- ☐ They may use formal and pedantic speech.
- ☐ They may have difficulty understanding non-verbal communication in others.

Notes

Play

- ☐ Some children with ASD have rich imaginations.
- ☐ They often play independently in one activity for hours (if the activity is chosen by them).
- ☐ They may have a tendency to collect, order and classify items.
- ☐ Their imaginative play tends to be solitary, and for some can be limited and repetitive.
- ☐ They may engage in memorized re-enactments of movies or television shows.

Notes

Academic Abilities

- ☐ Children with ASD have a wide range of learning abilities.
- ☐ They are often talented in understanding the logical and physical world, noticing details and remembering facts.
- ☐ Some children with ASD have phenomenal long-term memory abilities.
- ☐ Some children with ASD are hyperlexic, meaning they read much earlier than expected.
- ☐ They can be distracted easily in the classroom.
- ☐ They can be perfectionists.
- ☐ They can struggle with the mechanics of handwriting.
- ☐ They can quickly forget instructions or requests.
- ☐ They can have difficulty starting new activities.
- ☐ They can struggle to learn to read, spell, write and/or use numbers.

Notes

Movement and Coordination

- ☐ Some young children with ASD have excellent skills for solitary sports.
- ☐ Other young children with ASD have motor difficulties.
- ☐ They may be clumsy, have an unusual gait or have difficulty catching a ball.
- ☐ Some young children with ASD have fine motor difficulties (e.g. with writing and cutting).
- ☐ They may have low muscle tone and fatigue easily.

Notes

Senses

- ☐ Young children with ASD may be oversensitive to sensory experiences (also referred to as hypersensitivity or sensory sensitivity).
- ☐ The most common sensitivities are to specific sounds, but children can also be sensitive to touch, light, temperature, smell, taste and the texture of foods.
- ☐ When overwhelmed, they may attempt to block out their senses by running away, hiding or trying to destroy objects they think are causing them pain.
- ☐ Other young children with ASD are undersensitive to sensory experiences (also referred to as hyposensitivity).
- ☐ These young children do not notice a sensory experience (i.e. noise, movement or touch) until it is at a maximum. These children often need to move more and actively seek sensory experiences – for example, they may touch and lick objects, eat non-edible objects.
- ☐ Some children have both hypersensitivity and hyposensitivity. For example, they may be unaware of some sounds but be very sensitive to others (i.e. may turn up the volume of their favourite cartoon, but complain about other people talking too loudly).
- ☐ They may have high pain thresholds.
- ☐ They may not perceive the sensations of needing to go to the toilet, or of hunger, thirst or body temperature.

Notes

Special Interests

☐ Children with ASD may be intensely interested or focused on a special topic.

☐ Their special interests can be a source of enjoyment, knowledge, self-identity and self-esteem.

☐ Common special interests of young children include collecting objects and information on topics such as trains, planes, TV shows and fictional characters (e.g. superheroes).

☐ They may have difficulty disengaging from their special interest or knowing when to stop talking about their special interest.

Notes

Emotions

☐ Children with ASD typically have difficulties recognizing basic emotions within themselves.

☐ They may experience difficulty expressing emotions through verbal and non-verbal communication (i.e. showing emotions through facial expressions).

☐ They often show emotions in unusual or socially inappropriate ways (may use stereotyped behaviours such as hand flapping or specific learned phrases).

☐ They may have difficulty identifying and responding appropriately to obvious signs of emotions in others, and thus they may be misinterpreted as having reduced empathy.

☐ They tend to be more prone to feeling anxious, stressed and frustrated for more of the day, with a greater intensity than their peers, and to seemingly small triggers.

☐ They can move from 0 (no emotion) to 10 (extreme emotions such as rage) in a matter of seconds.

☐ They may not show, or be aware of, the early signs of rising emotions.

☐ It can be difficult to understand what has triggered the emotion of a young child with ASD.

☐ They may find it difficult to regulate their emotions.

☐ They can be resistant to conventional attempts to help them calm down, such as a hug or trying to talk through the problem. Sometimes these methods can actually increase their distress.

☐ A child with ASD may experience higher levels of anxiety than typical children generally do, to the extent that they may receive an additional diagnosis of an anxiety disorder including generalized anxiety disorder, social anxiety disorder, separation anxiety, phobias and obsessive compulsive disorder.

Notes

Summary

Over our many years of working with children with ASD, we have learned that it is crucial to have a good understanding of your child's strengths and challenges so you can understand, support and advocate for your child. Strengths and challenges experienced by young children with ASD commonly occur in the following areas:

✓ perspective taking (or Theory of Mind)
✓ social interactions
✓ communication
✓ play
✓ academic abilities
✓ movement and coordination
✓ senses
✓ special interests
✓ emotions.

What Is Anxiety?

Everybody, children and adults alike, experience anxiety from time to time. Most people think of anxiety as an uncomfortable feeling of nervousness, worry or tension. However, the feeling of 'anxiety' is only one component of anxiety. Anxiety is a survival mechanism involving thoughts, emotions, body sensations and actions. It occurs when a person is in danger (or believes they are in danger). Some of the symptoms of anxiety, such as increased alertness and more oxygen to the brain, can assist us to survive danger. So, although we might not like the experience of anxiety, we need anxiety!

Let's look at how these four components of anxiety work to protect us.

Thoughts

Thoughts are words or images that occur in our brain. When we are experiencing anxiety, our thoughts often involve predictions about something bad happening and judgements that (if we don't act) we will not survive or cope with this bad event. When we are experiencing anxiety, we may also see in our mind the bad event occurring or the aftermath of the bad event. These thoughts then cause us to feel the emotion 'anxiety'.

Emotion

This is the subjective feeling of anxiety. Anxiety is often described as an uncomfortable or negative feeling. Because the feeling of anxiety is uncomfortable, we are often motivated to get rid of it (or its cause) by taking action.

Body Signs

Body signs are the physical sensations we notice when our bodies signal to us that there may be a threat present and that we may need to take action. These changes are automatically triggered by feelings of fear or the presence of a perceived threat and are often referred to as being a part of the 'fight, flight or freeze' response. Body changes involved in the 'fight, flight or freeze' response include:

- increase in heart rate
- increase in breathing rate
- muscle tension
- sweating
- shaking
- tingling or nauseous feeling in the stomach (i.e. 'butterflies')

- dilation of pupils
- needing to wee, poo or vomit.

All of these body changes prepare us to fight the danger, flee the danger or freeze (to avoid detection by the danger).

Behaviour

Behaviour is the final step in anxiety and refers to what we choose to do. Usually, for young children with ASD, these behaviours involve fights, fleeing (avoiding a situation by escaping it or refusing to enter it) or freezing (stopping all actions by not talking, making a sound or moving). Alternatively, behaviour might refer to attempts to calm ourselves or reduce our anxiety (e.g. by taking some deep breaths, asking for help, counting to ten).

When Is Anxiety a Problem?

Anxiety is a survival mechanism that has evolved in humans to help us survive life-threatening danger.

If a person is in a dangerous situation, the anxiety response is quickly and automatically triggered in order to alert them to danger and prepare them to act. For example, imagine your child is watching TV when suddenly the TV bursts into flames. Your child thinks, 'This is not safe, this fire could burn me and hurt me!' They then feel fear. Next, their body changes to help them prepare for action (e.g. their heart beats faster, their breathing gets faster, they start to sweat). Finally, they take action by running out of the room. In this truly dangerous situation, the anxiety response has worked quickly and automatically to help your child to stay safe. We refer to truly dangerous situations that trigger anxiety as 'real alarms'.

However, the anxiety response also occurs just as quickly and automatically if a person believes there is danger when in fact there is none. For example, imagine dropping your child off at school. You say goodbye and walk out of the classroom. Your child thinks, 'This is not safe. Mum is never coming back. I can't do this!' They then feel fear. Next, their body changes to help them prepare for action (e.g. their heart beats faster, their breathing gets faster, they start to sweat). Finally, they take action by running after you. In this safe situation, the anxiety response is not helpful. We refer to safe situations that trigger anxiety as 'false alarms'.

From time to time, all children will experience anxiety in response to a false alarm because they have not yet learned that the situation is safe, or that they can cope with it. Moreover, in small amounts, anxiety in response to false alarms can still be helpful. For example, a small amount of anxiety before an exam may motivate a person to try their hardest. Or a small amount of anxiety before a sporting event may trigger body changes that help physical performance.

But if your child *frequently* experiences anxiety in response to false alarms, and the anxiety is interfering with their life to the extent that they are often distressed and find it difficult or impossible to participate in day-to-day situations, then anxiety has become a problem.

Is Anxiety a Common Problem for Children with ASD?

Difficulties with anxiety are very common in young children with ASD. In fact, research shows that approximately 60% of children aged 1–5 years with ASD (without intellectual disability) experience anxiety to a degree that is problematic (Mayes *et al.*, 2011). Unfortunately, high levels of anxiety are also found in older children, adolescents and adults with ASD, suggesting that children do not simply 'grow out' of anxiety (Lever and Geurts, 2016; Strang *et al.*, 2012). Rather, children with ASD need help to overcome their anxiety.

Summary

✓ Anxiety is made up of thoughts, emotions, body signs and behaviour.

✓ It is normal to experience anxiety from time to time, and in certain situations anxiety can be helpful.

✓ Anxiety becomes a problem when it occurs frequently and interferes with day-to-day life.

✓ A 'real alarm' is a trigger for a helpful level of anxiety to keep the person safe from harm.

✓ A 'false alarm' is a trigger for an unhelpful level of anxiety that is out of proportion to the situation.

✓ Debilitating or unhelpful levels of anxiety are common in individuals of all ages with ASD.

When Do Children with ASD Experience Anxiety?

Many of the triggers for anxiety in young typically developing children also trigger anxiety in young children with ASD. Below is a list of anxiety triggers that are normal during the early years. Although it is 'normal' for young children to experience a small amount of anxiety in response to these triggers, young children for whom anxiety has become a problem will often experience large amounts of anxiety about these triggers, which impairs their ability to function on a day-to-day basis.

Activity: My Child's 'Typical' Signs of Anxiety

Read through the lists below of 'typical' anxiety triggers for young children and mark off triggers that apply to your child.

Common Triggers of Anxiety in 3–4-Year-Olds

- ☐ Loud noises
- ☐ New experiences/environments/people
- ☐ Books/stories/TV shows/thoughts about monsters and ghosts
- ☐ People in costumes
- ☐ The dark
- ☐ Being separated from a parent or caregiver

Common Triggers of Anxiety in 5–6-Year-Olds

- ☐ Books/stories/TV shows/thoughts about monsters and ghosts
- ☐ Media-based issues (e.g. wars)
- ☐ Being separated from a parent or caregiver
- ☐ The dark
- ☐ Natural dangers (e.g. fire, wind, lightning)
- ☐ Animals
- ☐ Being alone at night
- ☐ Getting sick
- ☐ Getting lost
- ☐ Noises at night-time

Because of their underlying ASD-related difficulties (as described above), young children with ASD also commonly experience anxiety in response to a range of other triggers (that most typically developing children do not experience anxiety about). Below is a list of triggers that commonly cause anxiety in young children with ASD. Later in the book we will discuss why children with ASD experience anxiety in response to these triggers. However, at this point we simply want you to start identifying which of these triggers apply to your child.

Activity: My Child's ASD-Related Anxiety Triggers

Read through the lists below of ASD-related anxiety triggers for young children and mark off triggers that apply to your child.

Changes and Transitions

It is extremely common for change of any kind to trigger anxiety in young children with ASD. The change may be related to the environment, routine, setting or people who work with/care for the child. Transitioning from activity to activity, from situation to situation or between educational/care setting also commonly trigger anxiety in children with ASD.

My child becomes anxious in response to:

- ☐ Small changes in routine (i.e. driving home from school a different way)
- ☐ Bigger changes in routine (i.e. attending a 'Sport Day' or other special non-routine day at school)
- ☐ Changes to their environment (i.e. furniture)
- ☐ Changes in the physical appearance of important people (i.e. a favourite uncle growing a beard)
- ☐ Change to education or care staff (i.e. having a relief teacher)
- ☐ Transitioning between activities (i.e. change from activity to activity at kindergarten)
- ☐ Transitioning between situations (i.e. transitioning from school to home in the afternoon), even to preferred activities
- ☐ Transitioning between settings (i.e. changing classes at the beginning of the school year)

- ☐ Trying new things
- ☐ Uncertainty as to what is to happen next
- ☐ Having a change imposed before their current activity is completed

Control

When we experience anxiety, we prefer to be in control of our own actions, behaviour and experience. However, children with ASD and anxiety difficulties are especially likely to experience increased anxiety if they believe that someone else is trying to control their behaviour or experiences.

My child becomes anxious in response to:

- ☐ Being told 'no'
- ☐ Being told to 'wait'
- ☐ Attempts by others to take control of a situation (e.g. others attempting to redirect the activity or others asking the child to change or transition)
- ☐ Attempts by others to deviate from the child's 'plan', whether that be their 'plan' of how a certain situation should unfold or their 'plan' for how the whole day should unfold

Sensory Stimuli

Small and large sensory experiences involving taste, smell, touch, sight and hearing can trigger pain and anxiety in young children with ASD.

My child becomes anxious in response to:

- ☐ Being accidentally touched by other children and/or extended family members and/or other adults
- ☐ Being hugged
- ☐ Wearing certain clothes (e.g. shoes, certain materials, tight clothes, jumpers, tags)
- ☐ Water being on their face or clothing
- ☐ Having their hair or teeth brushed
- ☐ Having sunscreen, mosquito repellent or moisturizer put on their skin
- ☐ Other tactile sensations: _____
- ☐ Too much background noise
- ☐ The noise of hand dryers, vacuum cleaners, school bells, fire alarms or lawnmowers

- ☐ Other noises: _____
- ☐ The smell of certain foods, damp buildings or perfumes
- ☐ Other smells: _____
- ☐ Certain types of lights (e.g. fluorescent lights or LED lights)
- ☐ Bright sunlight
- ☐ Stairs (because of poor depth perception)
- ☐ Other sights: _____
- ☐ Air temperature not being just right
- ☐ Body temperature not being just right
- ☐ Small amounts of pain
- ☐ Other sensory triggers: _____

Social Situations

Many young children with ASD experience anxiety in social situations. A social situation is simply any situation in which your child comes into contact with one or more people.

My child becomes anxious in response to:

- ☐ Meeting new people
- ☐ New people being nearby
- ☐ Adults saying hello
- ☐ Peers saying hello
- ☐ Adults talking and asking questions
- ☐ Peers talking and asking questions
- ☐ One peer trying to play with her
- ☐ Small groups of children (2–5 children)
- ☐ Large groups of children (five or more children)
- ☐ Large crowds of people (e.g. shopping centres, parties, concerts)
- ☐ Participating in group time at school
- ☐ Asking questions in class
- ☐ Separation from a parent who acts as a social and behavioural guide

Academic Situations

Learning activities as well as academic situations can trigger anxiety in young children with ASD. Although some of this anxiety is due to the social component of these academic situations, sometimes this anxiety is related to the learning activity or the demands placed on the child.

My child becomes anxious in response to:

- ☐ Writing activities
- ☐ Reading activities
- ☐ Cutting activities
- ☐ New academic tasks
- ☐ Difficult academic tasks
- ☐ Receiving criticism or corrections on academic work
- ☐ Making a mistake on an activity
- ☐ Perception that their work is not perfect
- ☐ Other: _____

Summary

Young children with ASD experience anxiety in response to 'typical' triggers as well as ASD-specific triggers including:

- ✓ changes and transitions
- ✓ control (or loss of control)
- ✓ sensory stimuli
- ✓ social situations
- ✓ academic situations.

What Does Anxiety Look Like in Young Children with ASD?

As we discussed earlier, anxiety involves thoughts, emotion, body sensations and actions. Although we can observe our child's actions, identifying their anxious thoughts, emotions and body sensations often requires them to talk to us.

Activity: Ways My Child Verbalizes Her Anxiety

Below is a description of thoughts, emotions and body sensations your child may be able to verbalize to you. Read through each description and mark off statements your child has made.

Thoughts

- ☐ I don't want to go there.
- ☐ That dog is going to bite me.
- ☐ I am going to fall off.
- ☐ I can't do this.
- ☐ It's too hard.
- ☐ I don't like this.
- ☐ I don't know what is going to happen.
- ☐ Other thoughts: _____ .

Feelings

- ☐ I'm scared.
- ☐ I'm nervous.
- ☐ I'm shy.
- ☐ I'm worried.
- ☐ I'm stressed.
- ☐ Other feelings: _____ .

Body Sensations

- ☐ I feel sick.
- ☐ I have butterflies in my tummy.
- ☐ My legs hurt.
- ☐ My chest hurts.
- ☐ Other body sensations: _____ .

However, in order for a child to tell us their thoughts, emotions and body sensations, they need to be able to recognize, interpret and verbalize their internal experience. This can be difficult for young children generally and especially difficult for young children with ASD. Many children (and adults) with ASD have a reduced awareness of their emotions, thoughts and bodily sensations, and therefore are not able to correctly identify and interpret their signs of anxiety. Even if they are able to recognize and interpret their signs of anxiety, they may have difficulty expressing them in words to us, especially when their anxiety is at a high level. Therefore, we usually know that young children with ASD are experiencing anxiety because of their *behaviour*. Their behaviour is usually a sign or expression of distress, a part of the 'fight, flight or freeze' response, an attempt to self-soothe or calm, or a sign or expression of a meltdown (extreme emotional distress caused by emotional overload, cognitive overload or sensory overload).

Activity: My Child's Anxious Behaviours

There are some particular behaviours that young children with ASD often exhibit when they are experiencing anxiety. Below is a description of each of these anxiety behaviours. Read through the descriptions of each behaviour, then mark off each behaviour that applies to your child.

Repetitive Behaviours

The term 'repetitive behaviours' refers to what used to be called 'self-stimulatory behaviours'. These are behaviours that are performed in the same way each time they occur. Repetitive behaviours include hand flapping, finger flicking, head banging, sniffing or licking. Repetitive behaviours are one of the core characteristics of ASD. However, when anxious, many children with ASD engage in repetitive behaviour to a greater degree in an effort to soothe themselves.

My child:

- ☐ Hand flaps.
- ☐ Finger flicks.
- ☐ Head bangs.
- ☐ Sniffs object.
- ☐ Licks object.
- ☐ Rubs objects on their body.
- ☐ Paces.
- ☐ Runs around in circles.
- ☐ Jumps up and down.
- ☐ Other: _____ .

And my child:

- ☐ Engages in these behaviours when distressed.
- ☐ Appears to be calmed by these behaviours.

Control

Children may try to control situations in an effort to stop something unexpected or anxiety-provoking from occurring to them. If your child frequently attempts to reduce their anxiety through control strategies, they may appear oppositional or defiant. Their demands may even start to dominate your household.

My child:

- ☐ Often tells me and others what to do.
- ☐ Gets upset when others do not meet their demands.
- ☐ States they will not do certain activities or enter certain situations.
- ☐ Sets the rules of the game when playing with others.
- ☐ Tries not to lose control of play activities by refusing to share toys with others or take turns.
- ☐ Appears oppositional and defiant.
- ☐ Controls our household with his demands.

Routines and Rituals

Many children (and adults) with ASD have a strong need for routine and may also engage in idiosyncratic or unusual rituals. However, when anxious, many children with ASD exhibit an even greater need for routine, an increased resistance to changes in routine, distress at changes in routine and more prolonged and elaborate rituals. Your child may engage in routines and rituals in an effort to self-soothe their anxiety.

My child:

- ☐ Has a high need for a predictable routine.
- ☐ Has rituals.

And my child:

- ☐ Has an even greater need for routine when distressed.
- ☐ Has more prolonged and elaborate rituals when distressed.
- ☐ Appears to be relaxed and soothed by routines and rituals.

Anger/Aggression (Fight Mode)

Children with ASD and anxiety can show aggressive behaviours as a part of the fight component of the 'fight, flight or freeze' response. They may become aggressive in order to be removed from an anxiety-provoking situation. They may also become aggressive because they are afraid and do not know what else to do.

My child:

- ☐ Hits.
- ☐ Kicks.
- ☐ Bites.
- ☐ Spits.
- ☐ Scratches.
- ☐ Yells.
- ☐ Screams.
- ☐ Other: _____ .

Avoidance (Flight Mode)

Most children with ASD and anxiety will avoid anxiety-provoking situations and refuse to participate in anxiety-provoking activities. They may also run away from anxiety-provoking situations. When they run away from or flee a situation, many children with ASD will choose a small, dark place to hide in.

My child:

- ☐ Avoids certain situations.
- ☐ Refuses to participate in certain activities.
- ☐ Runs away from certain situations.
- ☐ Hides in small, dark spaces (i.e. in cupboards or under beds).

Freezing (Freeze Mode)

Some children with ASD may exhibit behaviours associated with the 'freeze' component of the 'fight, flight or freeze' response. When a child is in freeze mode, they often shut down or withdraw and refuse to speak or move.

My child:

- ☐ Stops talking.
- ☐ Stops moving.

Meltdowns

Most children with ASD and anxiety will display 'meltdowns' when their anxiety reaches extreme levels. A meltdown is a display of extreme distress. Meltdowns typically involve tears, kicking, screaming and flailing arms. Sometimes meltdowns can also include self-injurious behaviours such as head banging or biting oneself. Children can be inconsolable during melt-downs. Meltdowns may last minutes or hours.

My child:

- ☐ Exhibits extreme displays of emotions which involve tears, self-injurious behaviour, kicking, screaming and/or flailing arms.

Special Interest

A way of blocking anxious thoughts is to engage in a behaviour such as spinning a coin or bottle top, or to engage in a special interest, such as collections of train engines or computer games. When observing the spinning coin, the ASD child appears mesmerized, seemingly enjoying their detachment from their surroundings. The special interest can be so engrossing and enjoyable that no anxious thought can intrude. By engaging in these repetitive activities, or special interests, the child with ASD is also avoiding social situations, one of the greatest causes of their anxiety. The enjoyment and escape from anxiety achieved by a repetitive, mesmerizing action, or by engaging in a special interest, can sometimes lead to an irresistible compulsion.

Sometimes, a special interest in superheroes and fantasy literature can be a way of coping with fears, with the child wanting the qualities of a superhero to become brave and fearless. The origins of the special interest may also be a way of overcoming anxiety. For example, a child who had a fear of spiders decided to overcome her anxiety by reading about spiders – knowledge to overcome fear. The more she learned, the more she started to admire spiders, and arachnophobia gradually became arachnophilia as she started to search for, observe and collect spiders, developing an expertise that was greatly respected by adults.

The child who has ASD can create and enjoy living in the relatively safe imaginary world of fiction or computer games, in which they are free from anxiety. This is a useful strategy, but needs to be one of many, so that the activity does not become the primary means of reducing anxiety. Unfortunately, if the special interest has become the primary means of effectively alleviating anxiety, any thwarting of access to the interest, such as preventing access to computer games as a sanction, will result in severe agitation, as the child may not have such an effective alternative means of alleviating anxiety.

There is another aspect to special interests relevant to coping with high levels of anxiety. Coping with anxiety is mentally and physically exhausting, and in the long term can contribute to feelings of being emotionally drained. Time engaged in the special interest can be re-energizing for children who have an ASD. The engagement in their interest is perceived as refreshing, a very effective and efficient emotional restorative when depleted of emotional energy.

My child:

- ☐ Escapes anxiety by using the special interest to 'block' anxious thoughts.
- ☐ Acquires knowledge to overcome anxiety.

Shut Down

When the level of anxiety is increasing and becoming intolerable, one option for a child with ASD is to 'shut down', to self-protect from being overwhelmed. Considerable intellectual and emotional energy has probably been consumed trying to contain and suppress anxiety during the day. The child desperately needs a coping and energy-repair strategy. An effective strategy is to become socially isolated, the 'flight' or escape response to high levels of anxiety. If it is not possible to physically leave her current circumstances, then it may be possible for the child to become psychologically isolated, perhaps adopting the foetal position and choosing not to communicate or engage with anyone, sometimes even falling asleep.

My child:

- ☐ Sometimes 'shuts down' when extremely anxious or exhausted from managing intense anxiety.

Other Behaviours

The child with ASD may have unusual or unique behaviours, actions and comments that indicate increasing anxiety, such as talking about a particularly ferocious dinosaur attacking a herbivore, or repeating fragments of conversation that were associated with the first time he experienced a particular expression of anxiety. Parents may find it valuable to create a 'foreign phrase' dictionary that translates the behaviour or phrases to identify the nature, type and depth of emotion. This is valuable information for all who care for the child.

Other signs of my child's anxiety (may include idiosyncratic signs of anxiety, e.g. singing, giggling or repeating a certain phrase or question over and over):

Summary

Some young children with ASD may be able to verbalize their anxious thoughts, feelings and body sensations. Usually, we can tell that a young child with ASD is experiencing anxiety because of their behaviour or changes in their behaviour. Anxious behaviours displayed by young children with ASD can include:

- ✓ stimming
- ✓ controlling behaviours
- ✓ adherence to routines
- ✓ ritualized behaviour
- ✓ anger/aggression
- ✓ avoidance
- ✓ freezing
- ✓ meltdowns.

What Is the Difference Between Anxious and Naughty Behaviour?

One of the most commonly asked questions by parents of young children with ASD is 'How can I tell if my child is just being naughty, or if their behaviour is the result of anxiety or ASD?' This is a really important question because all young children with ASD will, at times, become emotional in an attempt to get what they want. We refer to this behaviour as 'temper tantrums'. And they will also, at times, become very emotional when they can no longer cope in their current situation. We refer to this behaviour as 'meltdowns'.

Meltdowns and tantrums are not the same. Understanding the differences between these two behaviours can be difficult at times. However, being able to distinguish a meltdown from a temper tantrum is important because they have different causes and need different responses in order to manage them effectively and not create more problems.

What Is a Meltdown?

- A meltdown is an extreme emotional display that occurs because of anxiety, cognitive overload and/or sensory overload.
- It is an involuntary reaction in which a child has lost all, or almost all, control.
- During a meltdown a child's verbal and learning abilities shut down.
- Some meltdowns have a sudden onset and occur in response to an obvious trigger. At other times a child will show increasing signs of anxiety and agitation over a long period of time, then have a meltdown in response to a final (and sometimes small) trigger.
- Meltdowns will run their own course and will end in their own time; however, social and sensory reduction can help to calm the child down.
- Attempting to make a child stop their meltdown by using traditional behaviour management strategies (e.g. reminding a child of the consequences for misbehaviour) will be unsuccessful.
- Instead, strategies need to focus on emotion management.

What Is a Temper Tantrum?

- A temper tantrum is the result of a child not getting his own way.
- A common trigger for temper tantrums is the word 'no'.
- Often children voluntarily choose to have temper tantrums and remain

in control of their behaviour. However, during a tantrum a child may escalate to the point where their emotions take over and they lose control. In this way, a tantrum can escalate into a meltdown.

- Usually, as soon as the child is given their own way, the temper tantrum will stop; it is like an on/off switch.
- A child may have a tantrum in an effort to avoid entering an anxiety-provoking situation.
- Strategies for temper tantrums need to focus on behaviour management (i.e. using rewards for desirable behaviour and natural or other consequences for undesirable behaviours).

Summary

All young children with ASD display both temper tantrums and meltdowns. Temper tantrums occur when a child is not getting their own way. Meltdowns occur when a child is experiencing extremely high levels of anxiety, cognitive overload or sensory overload. It is important to be able to distinguish between your child's tantrum and meltdown behaviours because they require different responses in order to be managed effectively.

Activity: Setting My Goals

It is important to know what you are hoping to achieve by the end of the *Fun with Feelings* programme; not only will you have a greater chance of achieving it, but you will also be able to track your progress. Write down what you hope for your child as a result of completing this programme. First, write down your general goal. For example, you may hope that your child will be able to manage their anxiety better. This is a great general goal.

My general goal is:

Next think about *how you would know* if you had achieved that goal. A good way of doing this is to imagine that you wake up tomorrow morning and magically your goal has been met. How would you know? What would your child be doing differently?

Now write down a more specific goal – that is, make your goal a SMART[1] goal (Doran, 1981). A SMART goal is one that is: Specific, Measurable, Attainable, Realistic and Time-limited.

- ✓ **Specific:** Choose only *one clear observable behaviour* you wish for your child to decrease or increase. For example: banging his head on the wall, asking an adult for help, attending kindergarten, or sleeping in her own bed.
- ✓ **Measurable:** The behaviour you choose must be observable so that you can measure it either in frequency or duration or intensity. For example: 'I would like my child to attend kindergarten *twice a week for half a day each time.*'
- ✓ **Attainable:** The goal you choose must be possible. Unattainable goals that rely on factors beyond your control are likely to fail. For example, an unattainable goal would be for your child not to experience anxiety. You can set this goal but you cannot attain it, everyone experiences anxiety, it is normal.
- ✓ **Realistic:** The goal must be within the range of your child's capacity, based on your knowledge of her developmental age and learning

---

1   For the origin of SMART goals see: www.projectsmart.co.uk/brief-history-of-smart-goals.php

capacity. Children are not miniature adults, and it is perfectly normal for children to experience meltdowns and emotion dysregulation, even if they are developing typically and do not have ASD. An unrealistic goal would be for your child to stop experiencing anxiety and meltdowns.

✓ **Time-limited:** It is helpful to set a time period within which you would like to achieve the goal. This parameter helps to prevent a scenario where we keep trying the same strategies over and over to no good effect. We need time to stop, to evaluate what we are doing and whether it is working, to examine the possible barriers to change, and to set new goals if needed.

An example of a SMART goal is:

My child will experience 'meltdowns' (defined as hitting, kicking and/or screaming) (**Specific**) once or twice per week, instead of once or twice daily (**Measurable, Attainable, Realistic**), and the meltdowns will be of shorter duration (i.e. 10–20 minutes instead of one hour) (**Measurable**) by the end of this ten-step programme, which I will complete in ten weeks (**Time-limited**).

My SMART goal is:

Weekly Plan Stage 1

The goal of the Weekly Plan for Stage 1 is to increase your awareness of your child's signs of anxiety and triggers for anxiety, and to increase your ability to distinguish between your child's meltdowns and temper tantrums. In order to achieve this, you need to record your child's triggers, signs of and responses to anxiety as well as their behavioural patterns.

However, keep in mind that it can be really difficult to tease apart the difference between a meltdown and a temper tantrum, and at times a temper tantrum can turn into a meltdown. Sometimes you will get it right and other times you won't. That is OK! Parenting is all about learning on the job and everyone makes mistakes.

Action

This week keep a record of your child's anxiety and your response to their anxiety by recording:

- ✓ What triggered your child's anxiety.
- ✓ The signs of anxiety you noticed in your child.
- ✓ How much anxiety you think they experienced on a 0–10 scale.
- ✓ If they had a meltdown.
- ✓ How you responded to the anxiety and meltdowns.

Use the forms provided on the next pages, entitled "Record of Meltdowns and Tantrums" for Stage 1 to record this information. Once you have monitored your child's meltdowns and temper tantrums for a week, complete the questions at the end of the chapter.

To get the most out of this activity:

✓ Keep a copy of the form handy.
✓ Complete the form as soon as is possible after an emotional episode.
✓ Describe as much detail as you can.

Frequently Asked Questions

**Our days are so busy, what if I don't have time to complete
the 'meltdown/temper tantrum' monitoring form?**
Life can get very busy sometimes, and adding another task to an already jam-packed day can seem overwhelming. However, in order to learn the difference between your child's meltdowns and temper tantrums, it is essential to get some realistic information (i.e. accurate data). Otherwise, we can easily believe the problem happens all the time and it is completely unmanageable. Also, having an awareness of differences between your child's meltdowns and temper tantrums will allow you to quickly and confidently select strategies to manage her behaviour. Thus, in the long term you will actually save time.

**Is it OK to compete the monitoring sheet at the end of the day
rather than straight after a meltdown or temper tantrum?**
It is preferable to take data on your child's behaviour straight after the event. We find data compiled straight after the event is often more detailed and accurate. However, if you really can't complete the form straight after the event, try to complete it as soon as possible.

Record of Meltdowns and Tantrums

Day/time/place	Triggers	Signs of anxiety	Level of anxiety (small, medium, big)	Meltdown or tantrum (and duration)	How you responded
Example: Saturday morning, before swimming lesson, at home	Change of routine – needed to take black car as my husband had the grey car Brother had two friends over playing Xbox loudly – sensory overload	Flicking fingers beside eyes Refusing to go in black car Crying	Big	Yes, 10 minutes	Called husband to bring grey car home

Record of Meltdowns and Tantrums

Day/time/place	Triggers	Signs of anxiety	Level of anxiety (small, medium, big)	Meltdown and tantrum (and duration)	How you responded

Activity: What Are the Differences Between Meltdowns and Temper Tantrums in My Child?

An example of a meltdown my child experienced this week:

Trigger	My child's face and body looked like:	My child's actions were:	I responded by:	My child was calmed by:

An example of a tantrum my child had this week:

Trigger	My child's face and body looked like:	My child's actions were:	I responded by:	My child was calmed by:

How does my child's face and body differ between meltdowns and tantrums?

\---

\---

\---

\---

\---

\---

How does my child's actions differ between meltdowns and tantrums?

\---

\---

\---

\---

\---

\---

How do my responses differ between a meltdown and a tantrum?

\---

\---

\---

\---

\---

\---

\---

What is different about what I do to help my child calm down during a meltdown versus a tantrum?

The Environmental Toolbox

Overview of Stage 2

One aim of Stage 2 is to help you to understand why children with ASD experience high levels of anxiety and why this anxiety does not decrease over time. In this stage of *Fun with Feelings* you will also learn practical strategies to adapt the environment to better accommodate your child's ASD differences and thus reduce their anxiety. These strategies form the Environmental Toolbox.

During Stage 2 you will learn:

✓ Reasons children with ASD experience anxiety (Part 1).
✓ The interaction between core ASD difficulties and anxiety.
✓ Introduction to the Toolboxes.
✓ Environmental Toolbox for reducing anxiety.
✓ The Weekly Plan.

You will need:

✓ Your monitoring sheets from Stage 1.
✓ This book.

Reflect on Weekly Plan Stage 1

As we described in the previous chapter, after you have implemented your Weekly Plan for each stage, you will be asked to stop and reflect on the things you did and learned as a part of implementing *Fun with Feelings* at home. Reflecting on what we did not only gives us new insights but also ensures that new learning is embedded in our memory bank as a part of a reliable knowledge base. Before we start the new learning covered in Stage 2, let's take some time to reflect on the things you did and learned as part of implementing Stage 1 of the programme.

In the very first Weekly Plan, we asked you to keep a record of your child's triggers, signs and level of anxiety, and answer questions about the differences between your child's tantrums and meltdowns.

How often did you monitor your child's anxiety?

What were the challenges you faced when completing the anxiety monitoring forms? Where there any barriers that stopped you from competing the forms?

Top Tip

Check back to the FAQs in Stage 1 on pages 41–42 for tips on overcoming challenges commonly experienced when completing the anxiety monitoring forms.

Did you notice any patterns in the triggers for your child's anxiety?

What were your child's anxious behaviours?

Did your child's anxiety and behaviour differ depending on how you responded to your child?

Did you learn any new information about how your child appears when they are having a tantrum compared with when they are in a meltdown? Did you learn any new information about how your child responds to you when they are having a tantrum versus a meltdown?

Top Tip

We often find that completing the behaviour monitoring form can assist parents to feel more competent and confident in determining whether their child is engaging in a meltdown or tantrum. However, do not be alarmed if your confidence has not yet increased following one week of behaviour monitoring. As the saying goes, 'practice makes perfect', and your confidence and ability will continue to grow as you complete this task over time.

Activity: Anxiety Survival Plan

In Appendix A is your Anxiety Survival Plan. After completing the *Fun with Feelings* programme, this Anxiety Survival Plan can become a quick guide for anyone who is involved in your child's care to use to identify and manage your child's anxiety effectively. On this Survival Plan is a thermometer with room for you to write your child's anxiety triggers and signs (behaviours), as well as helpful strategies for reducing anxiety when your child is experiencing small, medium and large levels of anxiety. At the completion of this programme you will be armed with a wealth of knowledge about the triggers for anxiety for your child, their signs of anxiety and strategies for managing each level of anxiety. In the final chapter you will be prompted to add this knowledge to your Anxiety Survival Plan. This will be invaluable knowledge for home, school and therapy settings.

Let's start this plan now, using your Record of Meltdowns and Tantrums from Stage 1. Look at these sheets now and write into the Anxiety Survival Plan (Appendix A) the signs and triggers for each level of your child's anxiety.

Top Tip

It may be difficult initially to determine your child's triggers and signs of anxiety. Be patient and observant. Talk about this with other people who care for your child. Sometimes the triggers and signs are not obvious at first, or they may be somewhat unusual. For example, we know of one child who hummed the theme song for the old television programme *Gilligan's Island* whenever she had to leave the house to go shopping or to school. The song is about leaving safety, becoming shipwrecked and never being able to get home again. This was her fear and the reason for her extreme anxiety about leaving the house. She was non-verbal at the time and could not communicate the reason for her fear until she was an adult.

Anxiety in Children Generally and in Children with ASD

Anxiety and ASD are separate conditions that interact with each other. In the following table, we have listed factors that may lead to anxiety becoming a problem and staying a problem in children generally, and those that commonly lead to anxiety problems for children with ASD.

Reasons for anxiety problems generally	Reasons for anxiety problems for children with ASD
• Temperament • Avoidance • Assistance from parents and other important adults to avoid anxiety-provoking situations • Lack of coping skills • Parents experiencing high levels of anxiety, stress or depression • Parent and other important adults responding in unhelpful or inconsistent ways to child anxiety • Modelling of anxious behaviours	• Neurological differences in the brain • Differences in sensory processing systems • Communication difficulties • Difficulty accepting and adapting to change • Social skills difficulties • Parents and other important adults misunderstanding ASD • Parents also having ASD

Reasons for Anxiety Problems for Children with ASD

1. Neurological Differences in the Brain

If we look at the brain, there are some important structures that are involved in anxiety. One of those structures is called the amygdala, and the brain has two. The amygdalae play a role in the generation and expression of emotions, particularly emotions such as fear or anxiety. In other words, this is the part of the brain where the anxiety response is triggered. Another part of the brain that is involved is the frontal cortex. This part of the brain helps us to recognize and regulate our emotions. In young children with ASD there can be two brain differences relevant to strong emotions. First, the amygdalae are often enlarged (Ecker, 2017), so your child will experience high levels of anxiety in reaction to seemingly small triggers. Second, the amygdalae and the frontal cortex parts of the brain are often not well connected (Ecker, 2017), which results in your child experiencing difficulty in both recognizing her anxiety and in using strategies to calm down.

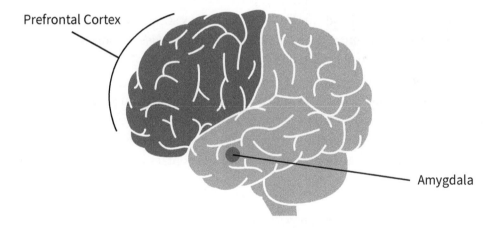

A metaphor to help understand the function of the amygdalae and anxiety is that of a vehicle being driven on a motorway. The frontal lobes of the brain are the driver, who makes executive decisions on what to do, where to go, etc. The amygdalae function as the part on the dashboard of the car that provides the driver with warning signals regarding the temperature of the engine. In the case of young children who have autism, this part of the dashboard is not functioning with the degree of sensitivity of a typical emotion temperature gauge. Information on the increasing emotional heat and functioning of the engine (emotion and stress levels) are not available to the driver as a warning of impending breakdown and the need to 'cool down'. If the child is unaware of internal emotional states, then anxiety will be very difficult to regulate. In autism, the dysfunction of the amygdala can also be expressed as a tendency to have a catastrophic emotional reaction at a relatively low threshold, pushing the 'panic button' too quickly. Typically developing children recognize signs of increasing anxiety much earlier and at a less intense level, and so are more easily able to manage it.

2. Different Sensory Processing Systems and Anxiety

As we mentioned in Stage 1, many children with ASD have differences in their sensory processing systems.

Hypersensitivity and anxiety

Some children are overly sensitive, or hypersensitive, to sensory stimuli such as noise, light, touch or temperature. These children are too sensitive to these sensory stimuli and can experience sensory stimuli as uncomfortable, painful or even extremely painful. If a child experiences sensory stimuli as uncomfortable, painful or extremely painful, he may:

- feel anxious about entering situations where painful sensory experiences have occurred in the past
- worry about when the next painful sensory experience will occur
- become more anxious about coming into contact with sensory stimuli over time.

Interplay between anxiety and hypersensitivity

Anxiety increases sensory sensitivity. For a young child with ASD and sensory sensitivities, this means that when he anticipates he will come in contact with a sensory stimuli (e.g. a noise, smell or taste) that has caused him pain in the past, he experiences anxiety. This anxiety then increases his sensory hypersensitivity, which in turn further increases the pain he experiences when he does encounter the sensory stimuli. This also means that layered sensory and anxious experiences – for example, anxiety about the noise and social aspects of a busy classroom – can escalate into a meltdown.

Hyposensitivity and anxiety

Some children with ASD are undersensitive (or hyposensitive) to sensory stimuli. These children are undersensitive to sensory experiences and may seek out sensory stimuli. These children often need to move more, like to touch and lick objects, eat non-edible objects and don't hear certain sounds. If a child is undersensitive to sensory experiences, she may:

- feel anxious about situations in which she is not allowed to seek the sensory input that she needs
- feel anxious about being reprimanded for seeking sensory sensations.

3. Communication Abilities and Anxiety

Children with ASD struggle to understand non-verbal communication (which accounts for up to 90% of our communication). This lack of understanding may lead children to:

- feel that other people are very confusing and unpredictable
- feel anxious when they are with other people.

Some children with ASD also have expressive and/or receptive language difficulties. If your child is having difficulty expressing himself to others or having difficulty understanding what others are trying to communicate to him, he may:

- feel anxious when others cannot understand him
- feel anxious when he cannot understand others
- need more time to process what others have said
- feel anxious when people reprimand him for taking too long to respond to verbal instructions.

Many children with ASD (with and without receptive language difficulties) have a specific difficulty with interpreting the meaning of non-literal phrases. This difficulty may lead children to:

- interpret phrases literally (e.g. 'pull your socks up' or 'in a jam' or 'break a leg')
- feel confused by others
- feel anxiety when communicating with others.

Interplay between anxiety and communication abilities

For most people, the language and communication parts of the brain shut down during episodes of moderate to high anxiety. This means that when children with ASD and communication difficulties are experiencing high levels of anxiety, their communication difficulties will become more profound, which in turn will cause them more anxiety. This also means that even children without expressive and receptive language delays may experience difficulties expressing themselves and taking in information while in anxiety-provoking or stressful situations.

4. Difficulties with Change

Difficulty adapting to change is one of the main characteristics of ASD. Therefore, the overwhelming majority of children with ASD experience difficulties adapting to change whether that be changing from one activity to another during the day, adapting to changes in settings or routines, or adapting to changes in people or the environment. Children who have difficulties accepting and adapting to change may:

- feel anxious during transitions
- feel anxious about changes to their routine, environment or setting
- feel anxious about attending novel events (even events that should be fun for them)
- worry about changes that may occur in the future
- refuse to enter situations or activities that have changed
- attempt to stop change from occurring
- function much better when in a predictable routine
- have rigid and unchangeable thinking patterns.

Interplay between anxiety and difficulties with change

As children with ASD find sameness or repetition soothing, they will seek routine, sameness and predictability when anxious. This means that when experiencing anxiety about other triggers, children may become more insistent on following routines and rituals and more resistant to change.

5. Social Difficulties

Difficulty with social skills is one of the main characteristics of ASD. Children with ASD have difficulties understanding other people, understanding social rules and standards, and interacting appropriately with adults and other children. Because of their social skills difficulties, young children with ASD may:

- find social situations aversive, confusing and anxiety-provoking
- experience other children and adults as intrusive (e.g. adults offering too much affection or other children being unpredictable or suddenly changing the rules of the game)
- experience other children and adults as confusing
- feel anxious when interacting with children and adults
- have negative experiences with other children and adults (e.g. being excluded or bullied by other children or being reprimanded by an adult for breaking social rules the child did not understand). Because of these negative experiences, young children may feel anxious about social situations and worry about future social failures/mistakes.

Interplay between anxiety and social skills difficulties

For young children with ASD, social skills difficulties become worse when they are experiencing anxiety. Poorer social skills then lead to negative social experiences (such as being rejected or laughed at), which in turn generate more anxiety in the long term.

Summary

There are many reasons why anxiety becomes and stays a problem for young children with ASD. Some of the reasons we have discussed thus far include:

- ✓ neurological differences in the processing of emotions
- ✓ different sensory processing systems
- ✓ communication difficulties
- ✓ difficulties with change
- ✓ social difficulties.

How Will This Programme Help?

Helping a young child with ASD to overcome their anxiety can be challenging, but it becomes easier when you are equipped with knowledge of your child, his ASD profile, his signs and triggers of anxiety, your own responses to his anxiety and evidence-based ASD-friendly anxiety management strategies. So far, by using the *Fun with Feelings* programme, you have been increasing your understanding of ASD and anxiety, and combining this with your existing knowledge of your child. In the next section of the programme, we will begin to discuss strategies.

Introduction to the Toolboxes

In *Fun with Feelings* there are three different Toolboxes, each containing strategies that will reduce anxiety in young children with ASD. These are:

- ✓ Environmental Toolbox – environmental adaptations that decrease anxiety in children with ASD
- ✓ Parent Toolbox – strategies used by parents (and other important adults) to decrease anxiety in children with ASD
- ✓ Child Toolbox – strategies used by children with ASD (with the assistance of a parent or other adult) to decrease anxiety in themselves.

We will start with the Environmental Toolbox.

Environmental Toolbox

In the Environmental Toolbox we describe below some changes you can make to your child's environment, at home, day care or school, to reduce your child's anxiety. Remember that this list is not exhaustive and your child may have other ASD-related needs that need to be accommodated.

Sensory Tools

As described in Stage 1, some children with ASD are overly sensitive to certain senses. These children can experience noises as being too loud, lights as too bright and certain tastes, aromas and tactile sensations as being overwhelming. Other children experience hyposensitivity and are under-responsive to certain stimuli. As described earlier in this chapter, either condition can increase anxiety in young children. If you feel that your child has a very different way of perceiving the senses, we highly recommend consulting an occupational therapist. An occupational therapist can assess your child's sensory differences and help you to make appropriate adaptations to your child's environments. Although an occupational therapist is best suited to helping your child with their specific needs, the Sensory Tools we have found to be generally helpful include the following.

If your child is hypersensitive to certain senses

- For noise sensitivity, allow your child access to ear plugs or noise-cancelling headphones.
- For light sensitivity, allow your child to wear sunglasses or a visor, even inside.
- For tactile sensitivity, cut off tags on clothes, buy seamless socks and consider buying second-hand clothes for softness.
- Ensure there is a quiet space at home and at school where your child can go when they are feeling overwhelmed.
- Avoid busy sensory environments.
- If you need to take your child into a busy sensory environment (e.g. the supermarket), go at a quiet time (e.g. Sunday morning).

If your child is hyposensitive to certain senses

- Allow your child more time to play outside.
- Ensure your child has regular sensory breaks throughout the day to engage in activities that stimulate their senses.
- Give your child toys that stimulate their senses (e.g. musical toys, playdough or a trampoline).

Activity: Adapting My Child's Environment to Accommodate Her Sensory Differences

Below is a table containing common hyper- and hyposensitivities and recommended environmental accommodations. Read through the table and tick any adaptations you feel your child may benefit from.

Sensory Sensitivities and Possible Solutions

Type of sensory hypersensitivity or hyposensitivity observed	Possible Sensory Tools	My child may benefit from these adaptations
Oversensitive to bright lights (e.g. sunlight, fluorescent lights)	Sunglasses Hat Visor	
Oversensitive to noise (e.g. busy classroom, assemblies, hand dryers)	Noise-cancelling headphones Ear plugs Playing white noise through headphones	
Oversensitive to fabrics or clothing tags	Cut tags off clothing Clothing made from natural materials Clothing without seams	
Oversensitive to water, lotions or sunscreen on skin	Adjust water setting in shower Use sunscreen and lotion only when necessary and discover most tolerated products and means of application (e.g. roll-on or spray)	
Undersensitive to oral input and so chews, licks and eats non-edible objects	Chewable jewellery or tubes	
Undersensitive to touch and so constantly touches objects	Have object child loves to touch always to hand (e.g. in pocket)	
Undersensitive to movement and so is constantly on the move and finds it difficult to sit still	Movement breaks Trampoline play 'Move and sit' chairs	

Change Tools

Change Tools are tools designed to assist your child to cope with changes in routine and transitions from one activity to another.

Change tools for routine and transitions

Children with ASD experience less anxiety when their days are predictable. All children tend to manage better with routine, but this is even more the case for children with ASD. Creating a routine that is consistent from day to day and showing the child what is coming next can help manage background anxiety about change. We include below descriptions of six Change Tools and activities to make them. Each Change Tool has a specific purpose. The following list labels the tools, and then we describe each one in this stage of *Fun with Feelings*.

☐ Use a visual schedule to share the daily routine with your child
☐ Use a now–then visual to transition your child to a new activity
☐ Use a timer or verbal statement to provide advance warning of change
☐ Give information about change
☐ Use Social Stories™ (Gray, 2015) to help explain changes or new activities/situations
☐ Use a visual calendar to explain major changes in the week or month

Activity: Create a Visual Schedule for Your Morning, Evening or Whole-Day Routine

Use a Visual Schedule to Share the Daily Routine with Your Child

A visual schedule is a line of pictures (or words) depicting each major activity during a specific time period (e.g. during a school day, during an entire day, during swimming lessons). Children use a visual schedule to gain information about what is going to happen throughout the time period as well as to keep track of what has happened and what is going to happen next.

Visual schedules come in many different formats and can be made from many different materials. Visual schedules can use photographs, pictures, drawings or writing to represent activities and can be vertical or horizontal in orientation (see the examples below).

Wake up	Get dressed	Brush teeth	Make bed	Get the bus

Often visual schedules are created on computers, then printed and laminated (for durability). However, you can quickly create a visual schedule whenever you need one by drawing a list of activities and checkboxes on to a piece of paper or sticky notes. iPad apps are also great for creating portable visual schedules.

- Song
- Sounds
- Words
- Reading
- Play

When used consistently, a visual schedule provides certainty and consistency for your child. Visual schedules can also improve your child's ability to manage changes to their routine because they will feel comforted knowing they can use the visual schedule to gain information about what is going to happen.

How to make a visual schedule

1. Break down the time period you wish to represent with a visual schedule into several steps or activities. Remember to include all activities, even minor ones (e.g. going to the toilet), or breaks.
2. Determine the best format for your child's visual schedule. Younger children respond best to photographs or picture-based schedules that involve physically removing a picture from the schedule to indicate an activity is complete (see example 1 below). Older children often prefer a combination of words and pictures and enjoy ticking off activities using a pen (see example 2 below).
3. Create your schedule.

How to use a visual schedule

1. At the beginning of the time period, introduce your child to the visual schedule by explaining what it is, where it will be located, and how they will use it.
2. Show your child what they will be doing during the time period by pointing out each activity on the visual schedule.
3. Draw your child's attention back to the first activity.
4. Prompt your child to go to the location where the first activity is located.
5. Once the first activity is finished, prompt your child to go back to their visual schedule and either remove this activity from the schedule or check it off.
6. Prompt your child to check the next activity.
7. Repeat.

Example 1
A type of schedule that uses laminated photographs which have been stuck

on to cardboard using Velcro. After each activity is finished, the child places the corresponding activity card into the finished box.

Example 2

A type of schedule that uses pictures and words drawn on to a A4 piece of paper. After each activity is completed, the child places a tick in the check box.

Activity: Create a Now–Then Visual for Transitioning Through Activities

The Now–Then Visual to Transition Your Child to a New Activity

A now–then visual is a very simple visual schedule that shows only two activities and is used to help transition a child from the first activity (now) to the second activity (then). It shows the activity a child must do first and the activity they can do next. Now–then visuals are very helpful when trying to encourage a child to do an activity that she dislikes, or finds difficult or anxiety-provoking. In these cases, the 'now' activity represents the non-preferred/difficult/anxiety-provoking activity, and the 'then' activity represents a preferred or reward activity.

Just like visual schedules, now–then visuals can use photographs, pictures, drawings or writing. Now–then visuals are often created on computers, then printed and laminated for use, but they can also be created quickly by simply drawing or writing on a piece of paper. There are also several apps on the iPad that can be used to create now–then visuals.

| Now | Then |

How to make a now–then visual:

1. Decide on the non-preferred/difficult/anxiety-provoking activity you wish your child to complete as well as a preferred or reward activity. Remember, if this is the first time your child is using a now–then visual, make sure the non-preferred/difficult/anxiety-provoking task is only mildly non-preferred/difficult/anxiety-provoking for your child, to ensure he experiences success using the visual.
2. Determine the best format for your child's visual.
3. Create your child's visual.

How to use a now–then visual

1. Show the now–then visual to your child and explain each activity. For example, 'First we will practise writing; then we will play Lego.'
2. Once your child has completed the first activity, praise him and draw his attention back to the visual. For example, 'Great writing! Look, writing is finished; now we can play Lego.'
3. Provide the reward activity immediately after showing your child the visual.

Use a Timer or Verbal Statement to Provide Advance Warning of Change
Use timers and give your child multiple prior warnings before they transition to a new activity. For example, give your child ten-minute, five-minute and one-minute warnings that the current activity will be finishing and another will begin.

Give Information about Change
Anxiety about uncertainty is very common in ASD. For your child with ASD, variety may not be 'the spice of life'! One way of coping with this can be to give your child more information about upcoming activities, especially if the activity is new or unexpected.

Before the unfamiliar activity or event occurs, explain to your child (ideally with the assistance of visuals):

- when the activity or event will occur
- where the activity or event will take place

- why this is happening
- who will be there
- what they can do if they need help.

One word of warning is to be aware that this tool may not suit your child. We have found that some children's anxiety increases with more information. In this case, give minimal information about the event, and only give advance warnings close to the event. Closer advance warnings still give your child a chance to mentally prepare, but less time to worry!

Use Social Stories™ to Help Explain Changes or New Activities/Situations

Social Stories, created by Carol Gray, are short stories containing pictures, photographs and words that describe a situation, skill, achievement or concept. Social Stories can be used for a wide range of purposes from giving a child feedback and positive reinforcement for their achievement, to teaching a child a new skill, to preparing a child for a change.

When used to prepare a child for a new situation, a Social Story provides a description of what a child can expect to encounter in this new situation from the child's perspective. This description may include information about dates and times, the physical environment, people who will be present and activities the child will complete. Social Stories preparing children for new situations also contain guidance on the child's actions. For example, stories often contain information about how a child can access help, who they can access help from and how they are expected to behave.

Social Stories can be used to learn about emotions, and anxiety in particular. For example, Dr Siobhan Timmins describes how her son with an ASD was 'not able to identify calm in himself, which made it impossible for him to work out how to calm himself down' (Timmins, 2016, p.35). She created a series of Social Stories, such as 'What are worries?', 'What is feeling calm?' and 'What does calm down mean?' (Timmins, 2016). Typical children would probably not need to learn the answers to such questions, but children with ASD often do need explanations and guidance answering these questions. Below is a sample Social Story to assist a child to understand the concept of feeling calm. The story was written by Dr Siobhan Timmins and is included in her excellent book *Successful Social Stories™ for Young Children with Autism* (Timmins, 2016), which we highly recommend.

What is Feeling Calm?

Feeling calm is a good feeling. Feeling calm is a comfy safe feeling. Many people like to feel calm. I usually feel calm when I am watching my favourite DVD.

    Sometimes I feel calm when I am stroking my dog's fur.

    Other times I feel calm when I listen to my music with my headphones.

    Usually I feel calm when I feel my hanky.

Feeling calm is a good feeling. Other people like being around me when I am calm. At home I help myself to feel calm by:

    Feeling my hanky or
    Stroking the dog or
    Listening to music in my room or
    Watching my favourite DVD or
    Maybe doing something else

    Mum and Dad feel pleased when I am calm.

More information about Social Stories can be found on Carol Gray's website http://carolgraysocialstories.com or in her latest book *The New Social Story™ Book* (2010).

Activity: Create a Visual Calendar to Explain Major Changes in the Week or Month

Use a Visual Calendar to Explain Major Changes in the Week or Month
This tool requires the creation of a visual calendar, which is a calendar that contains pictures or words depicting major, often out-of-routine, events. Children can use a visual calendar to gain information about when an event is going to occur as well as how many days the event will go on for.

How to make a visual calendar

1. Buy a calendar, make a calendar by drawing on paper or make a calendar using a computer.

2. Choose a photograph or picture to represent the major event and stick this on to the calendar.

How to use a visual calendar

1. When explaining to your child that a major event (e.g. school holiday, school excursion, house guests staying) is going to occur, show your child the visual schedule.
2. Explain to your child that the event will occur in X days or X sleeps.
3. Each day, encourage your child to check the calendar, cross off yesterday and count how many days (or sleeps) until the major event occurs.

Example of a visual calendar

Monday Home	Tuesday Home	Wednesday Stay at Grandma's house	Thursday Stay at Grandma's house
Friday Stay at Grandma's house	Saturday Home	Sunday Home	

Activity: Using Environmental Tools to Manage Anxiety About Change

Now let's put all this together! In the table below, list the situations in which your child experiences anxiety related to change. Next, list the signs of anxiety you have observed. Now go back over the six Change Tools described above and list the Change Tool that your child may benefit from. We have given you four common examples to help.

Situation	Signs of anxiety	Change Tool
Fear of change to the daily routine	Ben, 5 years old, frequently asks what he will be doing today He becomes controlling if changes need to occur to the routine	Create a visual schedule for the whole day routine
Fear of transition between activities	Stella, 4 years old, refuses to stop water play at kindergarten to move to the reading circle	Create a now–then visual Provide advance warning of change
Fear of entering a new situation	Guy, 6 years old, refuses to leave the house to attend a birthday party	A few days prior to the event, provide information about the event Provide advance warning of the event Use a Social Story™ to explain the sequence and protocol of birthday parties
Fear of going back to school	Mia, 5 years old, asks repeated questions about when she will be going back to school during the school holidays	Create a visual calendar to explain the change

Summary

Some of the core characteristics of ASD can lead children to experience anxiety. The Environmental Toolbox helps you to adapt the environment to better suit your child's ASD-related needs and thus reduces their anxiety. Environmental Tools include:

✓ Sensory Tools
✓ Change Tools.

Weekly Plan Stage 2

The overall goal for Stage 2 is to use tools from the Environmental Toolbox to help reduce your child's background stress. Check back to the last activity in Stage 1 to rediscover the SMART goal you created and write it down here.

My SMART goal is:

_____

_____

_____

_____

_____

_____

This week, to further this goal, I will aim to reduce my child's background stress by using two new tools from the Environmental Toolbox.

Action

Choose two tools from the Environmental Toolbox to try this week – you can choose Sensory or Change Tools. Through the week, complete the monitoring forms provided to record your use of each strategy.

Below, tick the two tools from the Environmental Toolbox you plan to use this week:

Sensory Tools
Hypersensitivity (oversensitivity)

- ☐ Make environmental adaptations including _____ .
- ☐ Make a quiet space at home or at school for my child to use when he is feeling overwhelmed.
- ☐ Make a plan to avoid going to busy sensory environments (e.g. the supermarket) *or* make a plan to only go to busy sensory environments at quiet times.

Hyposensitivity (undersensitivity)

- ☐ Allow my child more time to play outside.
- ☐ Create regular sensory breaks throughout my child's day for them to engage in activities that stimulate their senses.
- ☐ Find toys that stimulate my child's senses (e.g. musical toys, playdough and trampoline).

Change Tools

- ☐ Use a visual schedule to share with your child the daily routine
- ☐ Use a now–then visual to transition your child to a new activity
- ☐ Use a timer or verbal statement to provide advance warning of change
- ☐ Give information about change
- ☐ Use Social Stories™ to help explain changes or new activities/situations
- ☐ Use a visual calendar to explain major changes in the week or month.

Frequently Asked Questions

How will I remember to try the tools from the Environmental Toolbox every day?

It can help to take some time now to consider what times of day will provide the best opportunities to practise the tools from the Environmental Toolbox. It can also be helpful to leave yourself some visual reminders around the house of the strategies you plan to use.

My child seems to get more anxious if they know more information about changes that are coming up. Do I still use the Change Tools?

For some children with ASD, more information seems to give them more to worry about. If you notice this in your child, some of the Change Tools described may not be useful and we encourage you to adapt accordingly. For example, you may find that using warnings to give advance notice of change is helpful, but giving information about change is not. Not all of the tools will work all of the time with every child with ASD. We encourage you to experiment, monitor and use the tools that do work.

Environmental Tools Monitoring Form

Day	Tool 1: _____ Used? Y/N	Tool 2: _____ Used? Y/N	Comments
1			
2			
3			
4			
5			
6			
7			

The Parent Toolbox

Overview of Stage 3

The aim of Stage 3 is to help you understand some more reasons why children with ASD experience high levels of anxiety and why this anxiety does not just go away by itself. In this stage of the programme you will also learn more practical strategies to help reduce your child's level of anxiety. These are contained in the Parent Toolbox.

During Stage 3 you will learn:

- ✓ Why children with ASD experience anxiety (Part 2).
- ✓ Parent Toolbox for reducing anxiety:
    - Communication Tools
    - Modelling and Teaching Tools
    - Praise Tools
    - Reward Tools.
- ✓ The Weekly Plan.

You will need:

- ✓ Your monitoring sheets from Stage 2.
- ✓ This book.

Reflect on Weekly Plan Stage 2

You will remember from Stages 1 and 2 that taking time to reflect on how we parent can be enormously helpful when we are learning new skills. As you take some time to reflect on the week, remember to be gentle and encouraging with yourself. Managing a child with anxiety and ASD is challenging; be kind to yourself for taking the time to learn new skills to help your child. You are being an excellent parent in doing this.

In the Weekly Plan for Stage 2, we asked you to choose two Environmental Tools to try during the week and to use the monitoring forms to track your progress.

Strategy 1 that I tried was: _____

What were the successes you achieved when implementing this Environmental Tool?

_____

_____

_____

_____

_____

_____

_____

_____

_____

What were the challenges you faced when implementing this Environmental Tool?

_____

_____

_____

_____

_____

_____

_____

_____

Strategy 2 that I tried was: _____

What were the successes you achieved when implementing this Environmental Tool?

_____

_____

_____

_____

_____

What were the challenges you faced when implementing this Environmental Tool?

Why Do Children with ASD Experience High Levels of Anxiety (Part 2)?

Let's examine some more reasons why anxiety may become a problem and stay a problem in young children with ASD.

Too Much Avoidance

Anxiety is a normal part of life. Indeed, children need to learn how to cope with and manage anxiety in order to learn and grow. But children can only learn how to manage anxiety if they are exposed to situations that cause anxiety. If children are not exposed to situations that cause them anxiety, then anxiety becomes a problem.

Why Do Children Avoid Anxiety?

Children naturally want to avoid situations, experiences or objects they are anxious about. If you are in danger, the automatic and appropriate response is to leave the dangerous situation. Similarly, if you were previously in a dangerous situation, the automatic and appropriate response is to avoid entering that situation in the future. For example, imagine your child is playing on the school playground when she kicks a ball into the middle of the nearby street. Your child runs into the street to collect the ball. As she reaches the ball, she notices a car coming towards her. In a matter of seconds, she automatically thinks, 'This is not safe,' feels fear and experiences physiological arousal (body signs for anxiety). She decides to run back to the kerb. As soon as she reaches the kerb, she thinks, 'I am safe,' and she feels a rapid reduction in her fear and anxious body signs, as well as a feeling of relief. In the future, when the ball is kicked into the middle of the road, your child, remembering her experience, avoids running into the road and asks a teacher to collect the ball. When she starts remembering what happened last time, she experiences a sudden rush of anxiety, but as soon as she decides to ask a teacher to collect the ball her anxiety reduces, and she experiences a sense of relief. In this situation, anxiety has helped your child to avoid real danger and survive.

However, avoidance becomes a problem when your child believes there is danger and really there is none. For example, imagine your child approaches a group of children on the playground. In a matter of seconds, he automatically thinks, 'These kids are going to do something bad to me. I can't cope. I can't do this,' and he feels fear. Then he decides to walk away from the other children and stand by your side. As soon as he walks away from the other children and stands by your side, he feels a rapid reduction in his fear and anxious body signs, as well as a feeling of relief. In the future, when he sees a group of children in the playground, he will avoid approaching them. When he thinks about approaching them, he remembers what happened last time and he experiences a sudden rush of anxiety, but as soon as he decides to stay by your side, his anxiety reduces, and he experiences a sense of relief.

In this situation avoidance has not helped your child. In this situation:

- Avoidance has taught your child that avoiding situations quickly reduces anxiety.
- Avoidance has stopped your child from learning that the 'bad thing' he feared is unlikely to happen. For example, the children in the park were unlikely to do something bad to your child.
- Avoidance has stopped your child from learning he can cope.
- Avoidance has stopped your child from learning that anxiety also usually decreases if he remains in a (safe) situation.

In a nutshell, children are motivated to avoid situations because avoidance quickly reduces their anxiety in the short term. In the long term, however, avoidance ensures that your child's anxiety continues because it stops your child from learning that what he feared is unlikely to come true and that he can cope in the situation.

How Do Children Avoid Anxiety?

Children can avoid anxiety in many ways. Some of these may be easily observed but others can be very subtle.

Activity: How My Child Avoids

Read through the ways that children avoid the situations they fear in the following checklist and tick those you have observed in your child.

- ☐ Refusing to enter a situation.
- ☐ Running away.
- ☐ Hiding.
- ☐ Refusing to attempt a task.
- ☐ Acting in an aggressive way (to be removed from a situation).
- ☐ Acting in a defiant or disobedient manner (to be removed from a situation or to have the feared task removed).

- ☐ Complaining of being sick (to be removed from a situation).
- ☐ Staying in a situation but refusing to participate.
- ☐ Saying she doesn't know how to complete a task (to avoid a feared task or to avoid making a mistake or to avoid receiving criticism).
- ☐ Other: _____ .

Activity: How We Help Children to Avoid Anxiety

As parents, we influence our children and they influence us. It is very distressing for us, as parents, to watch our children experience pain, illness, distress or anxiety. So when a young child is quick to show anxiety, a parent may act to reduce their child's anxiety because it is so difficult to watch our child suffer. Consider the following ways in which you may assist your child to avoid situations at times and check the ones that you feel apply to you.

- ☐ Removing your child from the anxiety-provoking situation.
- ☐ Removing the cause of your child's anxiety.
- ☐ Keeping your child away from situations that have caused anxiety in the past.
- ☐ Keeping your child away from new situations in case your child experiences anxiety.
- ☐ Completing tasks for your child.
- ☐ Assisting your child to complete tasks.
- ☐ Lowering your expectations for your child.
- ☐ Making decisions for your child.

Sometimes we need to protect our children, but often helping children to avoid their anxiety and over-protecting, over-assisting and over-controlling them will maintain their anxiety in the long term.

Learning from Others

Children learn much about the world by watching, listening and talking with their parents, siblings, friends and teachers. Sometimes people inadvertently teach children to fear certain situations or objects through conversations and modelling of anxious behaviours. Modelling can occur in many ways, including:

- Telling your children that certain situations are dangerous. For example, telling your child 'Don't touch dogs, they bite and hurt little children' may teach her to fear new situations.
- Excessively talking about your own problematic anxiety and anxious responses. For example, a child overhearing a parent say things like 'I am sure I am going to get really sick from those germs on that train, it was just disgusting' may teach a child to fear germs and trains.
- Acting in overly anxious ways in front of your children. For example, a parent who reacts to a new situation in a very fearful way may teach their child to fear new situations generally.
- Agreeing with your child's fear or talking excessively about their fears.

Inconsistent or Unhelpful Responses

Knowing how to respond to an anxious child can be difficult and sometimes even counter-intuitive. No parent is perfect, and at some time or another, all parents, as well as other important adults in a child's life, will react to a child's anxiety in unhelpful or inconsistent ways. For example:

- Sometimes reacting with empathy and understanding and other times reacting with anger and impatience. These inconsistent responses can cause confusion and increased anxiety for your child.
- Enabling your child to avoid safe situations they are anxious about. As we mentioned earlier, avoiding anxiety-provoking situations maintains anxiety in the long term.
- Excessively reassuring your child. Excessive reassurance can send the message to your child that there is indeed something to be afraid of and that they cannot cope by themselves. For example, if your child fears a meteorite hitting your house, constantly reassuring him that your house if safe may in fact send him a message that this is something dangerous that we need to pay a lot of attention to.

Activity: What I and Other Adults May Do to Accidentally Communicate Fear

Gently, and with kindness towards yourself, take a moment to reflect on the information you have just read. Ask yourself the following questions and make some notes.

Do I ever feel angry or impatient towards my child? (It would be abnormal not to have these feelings at times.) What triggers these feelings in me? How do I respond when I am feeling anxious or impatient?

How do I nurture myself when I am feeling angry and impatient? If I do not do this, what are the barriers to doing this? How would nurturing myself help me nurture my child?

Are there any situations that I help my child avoid? How do I feel about these situations? Are these situations dangerous for my child or is there another reason we avoid them?

How much do I reassure my child? Does it feel like an excessive amount of reassurance? Why do I do this?

Whenever you take some time to reflect on your own parenting practice, it is important to be gentle and non-critical with yourself. Remind yourself that you are doing the very best that you can. Reward yourself by kindly telling yourself that you are doing the right thing and are on the right track. You have never done this before. It is hard and can involve suffering. Speak kindly to yourself and give yourself encouragement in moments of reflection.

Parents' Own Stress, Anxiety or Depression

All parents will, at times, experience feelings of being overwhelmed, stressed, anxious or sad. This is especially the case for parents of children with ASD, because although raising children with ASD can be very rewarding, it can also be very challenging. It is normal to feel challenged. In fact, accepting these very normal and human feelings, and learning to handle them in adaptive ways, such as facing our fears, problem-solving difficulties or asking for help, we show our children healthy ways to manage emotions. However, if we continue to experience high levels of stress, anxiety or depression, we are at risk of:

- unintentionally passing on to our children feelings of anxiety, anger or agitation (these feelings tend to be 'contagious')
- responding inconsistently and inappropriately to our children's behaviour
- being less responsive to our children's needs
- teaching our children unhealthy ways of dealing with emotions such as avoidance, becoming isolated, not seeking help and expressing anxiety through aggression.

If you believe that you may be experiencing problematic levels of stress, anxiety, anger or depression that are going on for too long, we congratulate you for recognizing this. One of the best strategies that you can follow to assist your child with recognizing and managing her own unhelpful ways of dealing with emotions is to recognize and manage your own emotions in healthy ways. There are many excellent strategies for managing stress, anxiety, anger and depression. In Stages 5–10 of *Fun with Feelings* we discuss strategies parents may use. If you are experiencing such high levels of stress, anxiety or depression that you are finding it difficult to cope day to day, or often feel 'at the end of your tether', we highly recommend that you make an appointment to see a psychologist or counsellor who specializes in cognitive behaviour therapy. If medication may help, he or she will recommend that you see your GP. If you are not sure about your levels of depression, anxiety and stress, there is a good questionnaire that you can complete online: www.depression-anxiety-stress-test.org/take-the-test.html.

Summary

There are many reasons why anxiety becomes and stays a problem for young children with ASD. Some of the reasons we have discussed thus far include:

- ✓ too much avoidance
- ✓ learning from others
- ✓ inconsistent or unhelpful responses
- ✓ parents' own stress, anxiety or depression.

Parent Toolbox

The Parent Toolbox contains tools that help you to parent your child in ways that will help her to better manage her anxiety. There are four Parent Tools:

- Communication Tools
- Modelling and Teaching Tools
- Praise Tools
- Reward Tools.

We describe these tools and how to use them in this section.

Communication Tools

A child with ASD can have more difficulties understanding speech and communicating her thoughts when she is stressed or anxious. We find it can help to understand if this is the case, and to adapt how you communicate with your child when she is anxious. Communication difficulties generally fall into two categories: being able to understand what someone tells us, known as receptive language difficulties, and being able to tell others our thoughts and/or feelings, also called expressive language difficulties.

If you believe your child has expressive or receptive language difficulties, we recommend that you seek help from a speech therapist. A speech therapist can assess your child's difficulties and provide you with a detailed plan for accommodating and improving these difficulties. Whether your child has specific expressive or receptive language difficulties or not, we suggest parents, teachers and other adults adapt their communication with a child with ASD during stressful and anxiety-provoking situations.

Activity: Adapting Our Communication During Times of Stress and Anxiety

As a helpful activity now, list the situations in which your child experiences communication difficulties in the first column of the table that follows. Next describe the communication difficulties that you have noticed. For example, are the difficulties about understanding speech or expressing themselves? Many children with ASD experience both when they are anxious. Finally, choose a Communication Tool they might benefit from. Here is the list:

- Use an alternative means of communication instead of speech such as actions, gestures or pictures. For example, show your child a sequence of photographs of him completing these tasks in the order you wish him to complete them.
- Use clear, simple instructions.
- Give only one instruction at a time.
- Demonstrate what you mean if your child is having difficulties understanding speech.
- Give your child additional time to process and respond to your requests.

Situation	Communication difficulties observed	Communication Tool
Arriving at kindergarten.	My child finds it difficult to follow my instructions to put his bag away, then put his lunch box in the fridge and his water bottle in the class container. He looks at me blankly when I give him these instructions.	Give only one instruction at a time.

Modelling and Teaching Tools

It is important that, when faced with stressors, parents model brave and adaptive coping behaviours. Equally, it is important that parents discuss with their children brave and adaptive ways of responding to different stressors.

Knowing when and how to model and discuss brave coping behaviours in a way that is appropriate for your child can be difficult. Below are some examples:

Situation	Examples of brave behaviours to model	Examples of brave discussion points
Running late to school drop off	Take deep breaths Keep calm	'I am a little worried because we are running late, but I know how to handle worry. I can take some deep breaths to relax and my worry will become smaller.'
Being presented with new food	Try food Keep calm	'I am worried because I have never eaten this food before, but I know how to handle worry. I can just try a little bit and see if I like it and I will be OK.'
Going to a new doctor	Keep calm Ask for help	Before the event: 'I am really worried because we are going to a new doctor and I am not sure I have brought everything I need. But I know how to handle worry. I can ask for help. I will ask the reception lady and she will help me.' After the event: 'The new doctor was nice and the reception lady was very helpful.'
Seeing lambs at a petting zoo	Pat the lambs Keep calm	Before the event: 'I am a little worried because I have never patted a sheep before. But I know how to handle worry. I will calm myself with breathing and I will just have a go.' After the event: 'I was a little worried because I had never patted a sheep, but when I did pat the sheep, it was lots of fun!'

Activity: Show and Discuss Brave Coping in the Face of Stress, Anxiety or Worry

Take a moment to reflect.

There are times when I show my own worry or when I avoid situations. What are these situations? What do I say and/or do?

There are times when I cope well with worry and stress. What are these situations? What do I say? What do I do?

Praise Tools

Praise is a powerful tool that you can use to increase your child's coping behaviours and decrease their anxious behaviours.

Look out for situations in which your child already attempts to demonstrate brave coping behaviour. Next, make a conscious effort to immediately praise your child each time he shows or attempts to show his brave coping – for example, talking to new people, trying new things, separating from you.

When using praise, make sure it is specific so that your child understands exactly what he did right. For example, 'Good job, Max, for being brave and waiting in the waiting room while Mum talked to the psychologist' is better than 'Good job, Max'. Specific praise is a powerful learning tool that can shape your child's behaviour.

Some children with ASD do not appear to like or respond well to praise. This is likely related to the highly emotional tone of voice, facial expressions and body language that adults often use when praising young children. If your child does not like praise, try giving praise to your child in a non-emotional, matter-of-fact voice. Or try praising your child by writing her a Social Story™ which explains what she did well (see page 66). Also, remember that if your child disagrees with your praise, you do not need to get into an argument with her about why you think her behaviour was good and why she thinks it is not. Simply end the conversation with a neutral statement such as 'OK, I thought you did well but I understand that you don't agree'. It is most important for your child to hear you praising her.

Activity: When and How to Praise My Child

Sometimes when your child is experiencing high levels of anxiety, it can be hard to be aware of your child's brave behaviour. It can help to make a list. In the table below, fill in the current situations in which your child attempts to overcome and cope with his anxiety as well as his brave coping behaviours.

Situation	Brave behaviour
Bobby experiences anxiety when I hang the washing on the line in the backyard.	He stays inside the house and waves at me from the window.
Madelyn experiences anxiety about attending kindergarten.	She attends kindergarten all day, despite screaming at me when I leave.

Reward Tools

Rewards are another powerful tool that you can use to increase your child's coping behaviours and decrease her anxious behaviours. Older children and adults can understand how facing their fears and practising coping strategies will help them decrease their anxiety in the long term and thus often have intrinsic motivation to engage in challenging and at times unpleasant activities. But young children who are still developing their thinking skills and abilities to delay gratification can find it difficult to understand how facing their anxieties and practising brave behaviours will benefit them. Therefore, they can have very little intrinsic motivation to engage in challenging activities. Young children are much more likely to engage in challenging activities and practise brave behaviours for tangible, immediate rewards. Star charts or token systems work well for this age group.

How to implement a star chart or token system

Step 1: Think of a task you want your child to complete regularly. This may be practising one of the Emotional Toolbox strategies or a brave behaviour (such as saying hello to his teacher). Remember, reward systems are designed to encourage your child to more frequently complete tasks that he is already capable of doing. In Stage 4 you will learn how to break down tasks that your child is not yet capable of completing (e.g. how to break down the task of attending kindergarten for a full day for a child who cannot currently separate from his parent for more than five minutes).

Step 2: Decide on the rewards that will motivate your child. Rewards can be material rewards (e.g. sticker, stamp or toy) or activities (e.g. going to the park with Mum, baking a cake together or bouncing on the trampoline for half an hour). When deciding on rewards, it is important to keep in mind that what motivates young children changes regularly. One week they may be strongly motivated by a reward and the next week show very little interest in the exact same reward. We suggest you regularly (i.e. every week or every two weeks) re-evaluate and, if necessary, change the rewards you offer your child. A good time to re-evaluate is shortly after your child receives his agreed-upon reward.

Step 3: Decide whether your child will receive a small reward each time he completes the task or will save up stickers or tokens (e.g. buttons, counters, beads, ticks) to trade for a reward. If you decide to use stickers or tokens, decide how many tokens he needs to earn before he is able to trade them for a reward. Rewards work if they are delivered immediately, consistently and only when the desired behaviour is carried out by the child. Young children need to see results fairly quickly, which is why stickers and tokens work well.

Step 4: Create a chart or token board and introduce the reward system to your child. Explain to your child that each time he completes the task he will receive a sticker/token on the chart or token board. Then, after he receives the specified number of stickers/tokens, allow your child to cash these in for an agreed reward.

Activity: Setting a Reward System for Your Child

To help you start planning a reward system for your child, write down the tasks that you want your child to complete more often and how often she needs to complete each task before being rewarded.

Task	Number of stickers earned before child gets a reward	Possible rewards
Play in the living room alone while I have a shower	3	Going to the park Ice-cream £2

Meltdown Tools

The best strategy for managing a meltdown is prevention – that is, knowing your child's anxiety triggers and signs and using the other tools from the Toolboxes to reduce anxiety before it reaches meltdown levels. However, sometimes, despite your best efforts, your child will have a meltdown. It can be very difficult to know how to handle a child when she is having a meltdown. Many parents and professionals alike find these situations over-whelming and often are unsure of what they should do. A useful analogy is to become the voice of a navigational GPS in a car. When the driver has not followed the guidance of the GPS device, the automated voice does not criticize or pass judgement on the driver, but simply and calmly explains how to rectify the situation. It is important in a meltdown to focus on what to do, not on the unacceptable behaviour. Be the calming and reassuring voice of the GPS explaining what to do to recover emotionally and cognitively.

Here are our top tips for managing a child during a meltdown.

Do

- Have one person take control of the situation.
- Stay calm, be assertive and feel confident. Remember to keep the role of the adult; be firm and in control.
- Use a slow, low tone of voice and clear, simple, minimal words.
- When speaking to your child, sit to the side and look away from her face (i.e. mid-distance, to side and down).
- Keep your body language calm, not imposing.
- When giving directions, acknowledge the emotions, give the reason for a direction, then give a direction (e.g. 'I can see you are feeling really worried. You need a break. Sit on this bean bag').
- As soon as your child starts to calm down, provide praise and encour-agement (e.g. 'That was the smart and the right thing to do').
- Keep your child safe by removing anything that she might hurt herself on and anyone who is not needed.
- Ask your child to sit down.
- Give your child as much solitude as possible by giving her an area to herself that is quiet. If possible, create a permanent, quiet, calm space and call it a name such as 'Calm Space', to ensure your child understands this space is not a punishment place like the 'Naughty Corner' or 'Time Out'. Ensure other spaces are used for these.
- Appeal to your child's special interest (e.g. start a discussion or have your child make a list or sort her collection).
- Give your child an emergency/calming-down box (e.g. a box filled with twiddly toys, puzzles, trucks, catalogues, radio to listen to, stress balls or spinning things).
- Give a compliment (e.g. 'You are a very intelligent girl').

Don't

- Don't touch your child, unless it is a protective action to stop violence.
- Don't match your child's mood with your speech (i.e. stay low and slow).
- Don't threaten or use punishment.
- Don't try to turn the situation into a lesson – your child's mind is not available for verbal teaching while in a meltdown.
- Don't say 'no'.
- Don't talk about consequences.

Summary

The Parent Toolbox will allow you to parent your child in a way that helps to reduce their anxiety and encourage their coping skills. Parent Tools include:

- ✓ Communication Tools
- ✓ Modelling and Teaching Tools
- ✓ Praise Tools
- ✓ Reward Tools
- ✓ Meltdown Tools.

Putting It All Together

So far, we have discussed that the many reasons young children with ASD develop problems with anxiety are complex and multi-faceted. Knowing *why* anxiety is a problem helps us to understand *how* to help our children manage their anxiety.

On the one hand, we know that some of the core characteristics of ASD, such as difficulties with sensory processing, communication, adapting to change and social skills, can lead children to experience anxiety. Increased anxiety leads to increased difficulties in all these areas. Some of the early interventions you are engaged with will increase your skills in these areas, but this work is slow and cannot provide immediate relief from anxiety.

Generally, one good way to reduce the anxiety produced by having ASD is to remove or minimize the child's triggers for anxiety by adapting the environment to accommodate the child's ASD. We do this by using the Environmental Toolbox, including Sensory Tools and Change Tools.

At the same time, we know that anxiety is a normal part of life; children need to learn to tolerate some anxiety to grow and learn. Anxiety reduces in children once they learn how to cope. Children can only learn to cope if they are exposed to situations that cause anxiety. If children are not exposed to situations that cause them anxiety, then anxiety becomes a problem. The Parenting Toolbox is a set of strategies that help children to learn to cope with anxiety.

To sum up, children with ASD and anxiety need both accommodation/protection and exposure to anxiety-provoking situations in order to experience less anxiety and increase their coping skills. Knowing the appropriate level of protection and accommodation, as well as when avoidance, over-protection and over-accommodation are occurring, can be difficult. To decide if your child has the ability to learn to cope with an anxiety-provoking situation or if we need to use an Environmental Tool, it is helpful to:

- have an accurate perception of your child's ASD strengths and difficulties
- have an accurate perception of your child's skills
- have an accurate perception of your child's anxiety triggers
- be confident in your ability to assist your child to manage their anxiety
- be able to manage your own anxiety about your child experiencing reasonable levels of discomfort or distress.

Weekly Plan Stage 3

The goal for the Weekly Plan is to start using two of the tools from the Parent Toolbox.

Choose two tools from the Parent Toolbox to try this week, then use the self-monitoring form provided to record your use of each strategy.

Tick the two tools from the Parent Toolbox you plan to use this week.

Communication Tools

- ☐ Alternative means of communication including using actions, gestures, pictures and speech.
- ☐ Clear, simple instructions.
- ☐ One instruction at a time.
- ☐ Demonstrate to assist in understanding.
- ☐ Give additional time for processing and responding to requests.

Modelling and Teaching Tools

- ☐ Model brave coping behaviours.
- ☐ Discuss brave coping behaviours.

Praise Tools

- ☐ Praise current brave behaviour.

Reward Tools

- ☐ Create a reward system.

Meltdown Tools

- ☐ Use meltdown strategies as needed.

Frequently Asked Questions

How will I remember to try the tools from the Parent Toolbox every day?
It can be helpful to take some time now to consider what times of day will provide the best opportunities to practise the tools from the Parent Toolbox. It can be helpful to leave yourself some visual reminders around the house of the strategies you plan to use (e.g. sticky notes with the words 'praise', 'reward' or 'use calm space' on them). If available, also ask your partner or friends to help you.

Parent Tools Monitoring Form

Day	Tool 1: _____ Used? Y/N	Tool 2: _____ Used? Y/N	Comments
1			
2			
3			
4			
5			
6			
7			

Small Steps to Conquer Big Fears

Overview of Stage 4

The aim of Stage 4 is to teach you how to assist your child to begin to face their fears in a safe and supported way. You will learn how to create a plan, which we call the Exposure Ladder, for your child, as well as how to implement this plan with your child. The Exposure Ladder is based on a form of therapy called 'graduated exposure', a therapy which is backed by over 40 years of research.

During Stage 4 you will learn:

- ✓ Why avoidance maintains anxiety.
- ✓ Why graded exposure will help your child to overcome his fears.
- ✓ How to create an Exposure Ladder for your child.
- ✓ How to use an Exposure Ladder with your child.

You will need:

- ✓ Your monitoring sheets from Stage 3.
- ✓ This book.

Reflect on Weekly Plan Stage 3

In Stage 3 we asked you to choose two Parent Tools to try during the week and to use the monitoring forms to track your progress. Take a moment now to reflect on your experience of using these two tools, being kind and gentle with yourself, allowing that learning new skills can be difficult and frustrating.

Strategy 1. _____

What were the successes you achieved when implementing this Parent Tool?

_____

_____

_____

_____

_____

_____

_____

_____

What were the challenges you faced when implementing this Parent Tool?

_____

_____

_____

_____

_____

Strategy 2: _____

What were the successes you achieved when implementing this Parent Tool?

What were the challenges you faced when implementing this Parent Tool?

Review: The Role of Avoidance in Maintaining Anxiety

As we discussed in Stage 3, we know that when children avoid what they fear, their fear increases over time. Avoidance can be obvious, such as refusing to enter a situation or running away from a situation, or subtle, such as staying in a situation but refusing to participate or claiming not to understand how to complete a task. Sometimes parents and carers unwittingly help children to avoid anxiety. Avoidance is a problem for the following reasons:

- ✓ In the short term, avoidance quickly reduces anxiety about a situation or task and therefore children are likely to see avoidance as helpful.
- ✓ Avoidance stops children from learning that the situation or object they fear is only in their imagination (e.g. monsters), is bearable (e.g. receiving criticism from a teacher) or is unlikely to happen (e.g. getting badly bitten by a puppy).
- ✓ Avoidance stops children from learning they can cope with their anxiety.
- ✓ Avoidance stops children from learning that anxiety reduces by itself if they stay in the situation.
- ✓ Without this learning, anxiety continues and usually worsens.

Activity: My Child's Avoidance

In the table below, list the situations or tasks your child avoids, how your child avoids these situations or tasks, and the fear you believe may be motivating your child to avoid these situations or tasks.

Situation or task	Avoidance behaviours	Fear
Writing tasks at school and home	Says 'no' Refuses to start Says 'I don't understand' or 'I can't' Runs away	Trying new things Making a mistake Criticism
Being in the back yard at Grandpa's house	Refuses to enter Clings to me Tries to climb on me Runs away and hides	The dog biting or hurting him

Graded Exposure

Graded exposure is a therapeutic technique used to gently introduce a child to the experiences that cause him anxiety, giving him the opportunity to use his coping skills. Starting with situations that trigger the least amount of anxiety, a child enters and stays in a situation until his already low level of anxiety is significantly reduced (this usually takes 20–30 minutes). He then does this repeatedly until he experiences no or very minimal anxiety about entering the situation.

Alternatively, if the child fears a task (rather than a situation he can stay in), the child repeatedly completes the task (or a part of the task) until he experiences no anxiety or very minimal anxiety about completing the task. In this way, we do not 'flood' the child with large amounts of anxiety all at once, but instead we build on success by helping him face his anxiety in small, achievable steps. Graded exposure is a well-established technique backed by many years of research. Graded exposure decreases children's anxiety because it teaches them:

- that their fear is only in their imagination (e.g. monsters), is bearable (e.g. becoming sick) or is unlikely to happen (e.g. parent never returning)
- that they can cope with their anxiety
- that their anxiety reduces if they stay in a situation long enough or if they engage in a specific task enough times.

Moreover, because graded exposure involves a series of small steps that gradually increase in difficulty, children can have lots of small victories and never become overwhelmed by anxiety.

Anxiety, ASD and Graded Exposure

As we discussed in Stage 3, children with ASD and anxiety need both accommodations and exposure to anxiety-provoking situations to effectively reduce their anxiety and increase their coping skills. This means that children with ASD and anxiety will benefit from graded exposure; however, this graded exposure may need adaptations.

Anxiety and Fear of Sensory Experiences

As we discussed earlier, many children with ASD have a different sensory processing system that causes them to experience certain sensory stimuli as being uncomfortable, painful or even extremely painful. Because of this pain, they can develop intense anxiety about particular sensory experiences or about the causes of these experiences. For example, a child might develop anxiety about bright lights or about places where bright lights occur (e.g. large shopping centres). Research to date indicates that the heightened sensory experiences associated with sensory sensitivity do not decrease with increased exposure to those sensory stimuli. Because the sensory discomfort does not decrease, the child's anxiety about the sensory experience that causes the discomfort does not habituate (decrease by itself through exposure). Indeed, exposing your child over and over to sensory experiences that he cannot tolerate is likely to increase his anxiety, not decrease it. Adults with ASD describe that they learn strategies to cope with the sensory discomfort, and, armed with strategies to cope, their anxiety about sensory experiences decreases. Therefore, graded exposure, as described below, needs to incorporate Sensory Tools if your child is anxious about and avoiding situations because of sensory experiences so that she can learn that she can cope. For example, if your child is anxious about and avoids the playground at school, in part because of the pain associated with the bright sun, it is possible to help her overcome this fear of the playground by using gradual exposure and first eliminate her painful sensory experience by providing her with sunglasses.

Need for Routine

A child with ASD tends to cope and learn better when there is a predictable routine in his life and change is minimized. Changes in routine can be reliable triggers for high levels of anxiety. Should your child with ASD function better with a predictable routine, we would not recommend disrupting the daily routine to expose him to more anxiety. Therefore, creating a predictable routine is a Change Tool in the Environmental Toolbox. However, if your child is exceptionally rigid and his rigidity is compromising important developmental goals (e.g. he cannot tolerate you driving a different way home from school), then we would recommend gradually introducing small changes to increase his tolerance to change and assist him to develop cognitive flexibility.

Fear of Social Situations

Children with ASD can become very fearful of social situations, including school, for many different reasons. Just some of these reasons include noise, smells, unpredictability of events, inconsistency between teachers, learning problems, peer problems (e.g. lack of friends, lack of social understanding, verbal and physical bullying or rejection) and social overload (i.e. too many people). To reduce anxiety, we need to understand what a child is specifically anxious about. Understanding the specific concern(s) allows accurate targeting of this fear with graded exposure. Because graded exposure is a tool for decreasing a child's problematic anxiety about a safe situation, we first need to investigate if school is an unsafe situation for the child. A potentially unsafe environment for your child would include an environment where:

- there were no true breaks in the day so that your child could not have relief from sensory or social stimulation
- your child was being exposed to regular (i.e. daily or weekly) peer or teacher bullying and/or rejection
- there were no environmental adaptations to assist your child to manage sensory issues.

Learning and Language Issues

Some children with ASD also experience problems with their learning and/ or language skills. Their learning and language profile can greatly affect their capacity to learn and socialize. If your child is very anxious about a social or learning environment where they are learning to read, or there is an expectation for social communication, the underlying reason may be that they are struggling to learn and communicate. If this is the case, the difficulties need to be assessed and understood. Merely exposing a child over and over to a learning setting where his capacity cannot meet expectations will not reduce anxiety; rather, it will likely increase it. In this case, graded exposure would need modification to accommodate a child's learning difficulties.

Please note

For parents with ASD: Clinical experience has taught us that it can be particularly difficult for a parent with ASD to consider school a safe place because of their own, sometimes horrific, experiences of school, especially if that parent was bullied by students and/or a teacher. If this is the case for you, it is important to acknowledge your own experience, to be thankful that you can be protective of your child, to acknowledge that your child is having a different experience to you, although some elements will be the same, and to be open to the possibility of a different outcome for your child. Your child's experience will be different because you are aware and protective, can be an advocate for your child at school and can help modify the school environment, while assisting your child to learn to cope. If, to reduce your own anxiety, you remove your child from school in favour of home schooling in the early years, you may severely limit your child's capacity to learn, socialize and overcome anxiety.

Summary

Avoidance maintains anxiety in the long term. Graded exposure is an evidence-based technique that targets avoidance by helping children to face anxiety-provoking situations in a gradual manner. Graded exposure is suitable for both typically developing children and children with ASD. However, children with ASD may require specific adaptations to graded exposure to accommodate their ASD differences and needs.

Overview of Creating an Exposure Ladder

There are several steps involved in creating and using an Exposure Ladder. First, you create a realistic end goal for your child. Then you break this goal down into smaller goals or steps. Next, you order these steps from least anxiety-provoking to most anxiety-provoking. Finally, your child completes each step, in order, starting with the easiest step. Your child continues to practise each step until his anxiety about that step is significantly reduced. Once your child's anxiety has significantly reduced and he is feeling comfortable completing a step, he moves on to the next step. Each time your child successfully practises a step, he is rewarded for facing his fears.

Step 1: Choosing an Exposure Ladder Goal

Graded exposure is essentially about helping your child to approach rather than avoid her fears. So, to help select an appropriate Exposure Ladder goal, think of a situation or task your child both fears and avoids. For your first Exposure Ladder, select a fear that is significantly affecting your child's and/

or family's day-to-day life, but not her biggest fear. We want your child to have the best chance of success, so selecting a smaller fear can assist with her motivation to engage in the process and improve the chances of her successfully completing the Exposure Ladder. If your child has several fears, you can create a separate Exposure Ladder for each fear some time in the future. However, to set your child up for the best chance of success, do not try to tackle more than one Exposure Ladder at once.

You will remember that in Stage 1 we discussed setting SMART (Specific, Measurable, Attainable, Realistic and Time-limited) goals for *Fun with Feelings* to work. This also applies to Exposure Ladder goals. An example of a helpful SMART goal is 'Bobby will feel less worried about being without me (Mum) and will be looked after by his grandmother for three hours in the evening'. This goal is specific, measurable, attainable, realistic and time-limited. It is clear exactly what the parent wants to see the child do. It is also a realistic and attainable goal for a 4–6-year-old with ASD to achieve.

An example of an unhelpful goal is 'Bobby will not worry about changes to our routine'. This goal is broad rather than specific and time-limited, and it is not clear what behaviours the parent wants to see demonstrated. This goal is also not realistic, as a child with ASD will likely experience some degree of worry about change. A better goal might be 'On four out of five days Bobby is able to cope with one change to the daily family routine, without having a meltdown'.

Throughout the rest of Stage 4, we will provide two examples to help illustrate the steps involved in making an Exposure Ladder. One of these steps will involve a situation, and the other example will involve a task.

- Example Goal 1: Noah will complete a grocery shopping trip (approximately 30 minutes) with his younger brother and me.
- Example Goal 2: Susan will complete a two-minute 'show and tell' in front of her class.

Write down your child's Exposure Ladder goal:

_____

_____

_____

Top Tip

Look back to Activity: My Child's Avoidance on page 103 to help you to find a situation, object or task your child fears and avoids.

Step 2: Break the Goal Down into Smaller Steps

The next in step in creating an Exposure Ladder is to break down the end goal into a series of small steps or goals. Think of as many small steps as you can that relate to your child's goal and list these in the table provided below. Different goals will involve differing numbers of steps, but there should always be enough steps in the ladder to provide plenty of opportunities for your child to practise and reinforce their coping skills. Typically, somewhere between five and 15 steps in an Exposure Ladder is appropriate for most goals. The steps should also range in difficulty and include things about which your child is 'a little anxious' (i.e. experiences low levels of anxiety), 'anxious' (i.e. experiences moderate levels of anxiety) and 'really anxious' (i.e. experiences high levels of anxiety).

The steps need to address the 'who', 'what', 'when', 'where' and 'how' questions:

- who will be there
- what the child will do
- when she will do it
- where she will do it
- how long she will do it.

Situation example **Goal: Noah to complete the family grocery shopping trip with me and his younger brother on Wednesday afternoons**	**Task example** **Goal: Susan to complete a two-minute 'show and tell' in front of her class**
Steps: • Sit in the car outside the shopping centre • Inside the shopping centre near entrance • Inside the shopping centre near the supermarket • Sit on the bench outside the shopping centre • Inside the supermarket (not purchasing items) • Inside the supermarket (purchasing items and checking out) • Inside the supermarket with brother (purchasing items) • Inside the supermarket with brother (not purchasing items)	Steps: • Hold visual board with show-and-tell script on it while the teacher reads the script to one other child • Hold visual board while the teacher reads script to three preferred peers • Hold while teacher reads the script to three non-preferred peers • Hold a visual board while the teacher reads the script to half the class • Hold a visual board while the teacher reads the script to the whole class • Say show-and-tell script (three points) to one other child • Say show-and-tell script to three preferred peers • Say show-and-tell script to three non-preferred peers • Say show-and-tell script to half the class • Say show-and-tell script to whole class

Activity: Steps for My Child

Break down your child's Exposure Ladder goal into smaller steps. These steps do not have to be in order at this stage.

Top Tip

Remember that the steps need to be specific, just like the overarching goal, and they need to include the 'who', 'what', 'when', 'where' and 'how' questions.

Exposure hierarchy steps for my child

Step 3: List the Skills Your Child Will Need to Complete Each Step

Now that you have a number of small steps for your child's Exposure Ladder, it is important to consider the skills your child will need to complete each of the steps. This will vary widely depending on what your goal is; some goals may not require any additional skills (other than anxiety management). Once the necessary skills for the steps have been identified, ensure that you practise these skills with your child through role plays and rehearsals. It is important your child masters each skill before she completes the step.

Situation Example

Goal: Noah to complete the family grocery shopping trip with me and his younger brother on Wednesday afternoons	
Step	**Skill**
Sitting in the car	Nil
Inside the shopping centre near entrance	• Hold my hand • Walk beside me • Stay with me • Refrain from yelling inside
Inside the shopping centre near the supermarket	• As above
Sit on the bench outside the shopping centre	• As above
Inside the supermarket (not purchasing items)	• As above And • Refrain from pulling things off the shelves
Inside the supermarket (purchasing items and checking out)	• As above And • Walk beside the trolley • Stay beside the trolley • Wait while the groceries are scanned, bagged and paid for
Inside the supermarket with brother (purchasing items)	• As above
Inside the supermarket with brother (not purchasing items)	• As above

Task Example

Goal: Susan to complete a two-minute 'show and tell' in front of her class	
Step	**Skill**
Hold visual board with show-and-tell script on it while the teacher reads the script to one other child	• Stand still • Hold visual board
Hold visual board while the teacher reads script to three preferred peers	• As above
Hold a visual board while the teacher reads the script to three non-preferred peers	• As above
Hold a visual board while the teacher reads the script to half the class	• As above
Hold a visual board while the teacher reads the script to the whole class	• As above
Say show-and-tell script (three points) to one other child	• Speak at appropriate volume • Stand still • Face other child • Look at other child • Remember three points to say • Take prompts from teacher about script points
Say show-and-tell script to three preferred peers	• As above
Say show-and-tell script to three non-preferred peers	• As above
Say show-and-tell script to half the class	• As above
Say show-and-tell script to whole class	• As above

Activity: Skills My Child Needs to Complete Each Step

Write down the skills that your child needs to be able to complete each Exposure Ladder step.

Step	Skills required

Step 4: List the Environmental Tools Your Child Will Need to Complete the Exposure Ladder

As we discussed above, because your child has ASD, you may need to alter some of the situations in your child's Exposure Ladder by using Environmental Tools. Environmental Tools include:

- ✓ Communication Tools
- ✓ Sensory Tools
- ✓ Routine and Transition Tools
- ✓ Change Tools.

Situation Example

Goal: Noah to complete the family grocery shopping trip with me and his younger brother on Wednesday afternoons	
Step	**Environmental Tools needed**
Sitting in the car	Sensory Tools
Inside the shopping centre near entrance	• Quiet day of the week and time of day at the supermarket (e.g. mid-week
Inside the shopping centre near the supermarket	during school hours)
Sit on the bench outside the shopping centre	• Sunglasses • Noise-cancelling headphones • Visor or hat
Inside the supermarket (not purchasing items)	Change Tools
Inside the supermarket (purchasing items and checking out)	• Social Story™
Inside the supermarket with brother (purchasing items)	
Inside the supermarket with brother (not purchasing items)	

Task Example

Goal: Susan to complete a two-minute 'show and tell' in front of her class	
Step	**Environmental and Parent Tools needed**
Hold visual board with show-and-tell script on it while the teacher reads the script to one other child	Communication Tools • Fewer words and instructions Routine Tools • Visual schedule of when 'show and tell' will occur Sensory Tools • Quiet room
Hold visual board while the teacher reads script to three preferred peers	
Hold a visual board while the teacher reads the script to three non-preferred peers	
Hold a visual board while the teacher reads the script to half the class	
Hold a visual board while the teacher reads the script to the whole class	
Say show-and-tell script (three points) to one other child	
Say show-and-tell script to three preferred peers	
Say show-and-tell script to three non-preferred peers	
Say show-and-tell script to half the class	
Say show-and-tell script to whole class	

Activity: Environmental Tools My Child Needs to Complete the Exposure Ladder

Write down the Environmental Tools that your child needs to be able to complete each Exposure Ladder step.

Goal: _____	
Step	**Environmental Tools needed**

Step 5: Arrange the Steps in Order of Difficulty

Now that we have created a list of steps and corresponding skills required to complete each step, we want to arrange the steps in order of difficulty. To assist with doing this, we will use a Worried/Difficulty Thermometer, with a scale of 0–10, where 0 equals no anxiety and difficulty, and 10 equals extreme anxiety and difficulty. Place the steps in order of difficulty alongside the Worried/Difficulty Thermometer, starting with the easiest step and working up to the most difficult step. The first step should be something that your child can do already or can almost do.

Once you have put the steps in order, it is important to make sure there are no big gaps between steps. If there is a big gap between two steps, add another step in.

Anxiety Thermometer

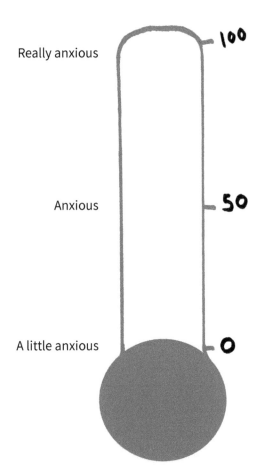

Situation Example

Anxiety rating (1–10)	Step
9	Inside the supermarket with brother (purchasing items)
8	Inside the supermarket with brother (not purchasing items)
7	Inside the supermarket (purchasing items and checking out)
5	Inside the supermarket (not purchasing items)
4	Inside the shopping centre near the supermarket
3	Inside the shopping centre near entrance
3	Sit on the bench outside the shopping centre
2	Sitting in the car

Task Example

Anxiety rating (1–10)	Step
10	Say show-and-tell script to whole class
9	Hold a visual board while the teacher reads the script to the whole class
8	Say show-and-tell script to half the class
7	Hold a visual board while the teacher reads the script to half the class
6	Say show-and-tell script to three non-preferred peers
6	Hold a visual board while the teacher reads the script to three non-preferred peers
4	Say show-and-tell script to three preferred peers
3	Hold visual board while the teacher reads script to three preferred peers
3	Say show-and-tell script (three points) to one other child
2	Hold visual board with show-and-tell script on it while the teacher reads the script to one other child

Step 6: Decide on Rewards

As we discussed in Stage 3, rewards are very effective in motivating children and changing their behaviour. Young children have low intrinsic motivation to complete Exposure Ladder steps because they struggle to understand how facing their anxiety and practising brave behaviours will benefit them in the long term. Therefore, they are much more likely to practise Exposure Ladder steps if they receive tangible immediate rewards.

Once you have finalized the steps of your Exposure Ladder, you will need to create a reward chart for your child. Because your child will likely find it very difficult to understand the concept of gradual steps on an Exposure Ladder, or the concept that by the time she reaches the higher steps she will be more able to cope, it is important that you only present one step at a time to her.

In order to establish the rewards chart with your child and link this to the Exposure Ladder, you may want to say:

> We are going to make a reward chart to practise being brave. This week we are going to practise (the first step of the hierarchy). Each time we practise (the first step of the hierarchy) you will get (a reward).

Or:

> We are going to make a reward chart to practise being brave. This week we are going to practise (the first step of the hierarchy). Each time we practise (the first step of the hierarchy) you will get a sticker for your reward chart. Once you get __ stickers you will get (what the reward is).

Remember, rewards do not need to be big or expensive. They can be anything your child enjoys. The most important thing to remember is that rewards are most effective when they are immediate. Therefore, rewards should be things that you can easily access or have readily on hand; otherwise, you may not get around to giving your child the reward.

It is also important that rewards match how difficult each step is for your child. For easier steps, your child might earn stickers or tokens that she can then cash in for a reward. However, for more difficult steps, there will need to be an immediate reward each time your child tries her hardest to complete the step.

Example Rewards

Rewards for easy steps	Rewards for hard steps
A small chocolate or other treat	A Superman figurine worth £5
An extra story before going to sleep	A day at the water park or beach
Stickers/stamps featuring favourite character	A new DVD
A short trip to the park at the weekend	Going on a family picnic
A small toy, trinket, pen or notebook	A massage
Extra 15 minutes watching favourite TV show or playing an iPad game	Access to a highly preferred activity for one hour
Card game (or other game) with Mum or Dad	

Activity: Rewards for My Child

Write down different rewards for your child that will assist in motivating him to complete his Exposure Ladder steps.

Rewards for easy steps	Rewards for hard steps

Summary

There are several steps involved in creating and using an Exposure Ladder:

✓ Select a SMART goal.
✓ Make a list of small steps.
✓ Identify the skills your child will need to complete each step.
✓ Identify the environmental adaptations your child will need to complete each step.
✓ Put the steps in order of difficulty.
✓ Negotiate rewards.

Climbing the Exposure Ladder

Now that you have a plan to gradually help your child face his fears, it is time to think about implementing this plan. Remember, graded exposure reduces your child's anxiety by teaching your child that:

- their fear is either only in their imagination (e.g. monsters), is bearable (e.g. becoming sick) or is unlikely to happen (e.g. parent never returning)
- they can cope with their anxiety
- their anxiety reduces if they stay in a situation long enough or if they engage in a specific task enough times.

For this learning to occur, your child needs to complete their Exposure Ladder step by staying in a situation until their anxiety significantly reduces (this usually takes 20–30 minutes). They then need to repeat this Exposure Ladder step until their anxiety about completing this step (i.e. entering this situation) is gone or is very minimal.

Alternatively, if your child fears a task (rather than a situation they can stay in), they need to repeatedly complete their Exposure Ladder step (i.e. part of the task) until they experience no or very minimal anxiety about completing this part of the task.

Therefore, there is no set number of times a child needs to complete a step; rather, they continue completing a step until their anxiety is significantly reduced. Also, there is no set frequency that a child should complete a step as some steps can be completed daily (e.g. saying hello to a teacher) but other steps can only be completed every couple of days or weekly (e.g. staying with Grandma). However, it is suggested that steps be completed as frequently as possible to help children consolidate their learning and progress more quickly. In the same way, if a step can only be completed every couple of weeks or less (e.g. going to a concert), it is probably not related to a fear that is impacting your child's day-to-day life and thus is not appropriate for an Exposure Ladder. Other tools from the Environmental, Parent and Emotional Toolboxes can be used in these situations.

To effectively complete an Exposure Ladder, there are some key points to keep in mind, before, during and after completing each Exposure Ladder step.

Before You Complete an Exposure Ladder Step

Prepare yourself, your child and the environment for the Exposure Ladder step by ensuring:

- You have created a reward chart for your child.
- Your child's reward is ready to be given to them as soon as they complete the step.
- You have explained to your child the reward chart and the Exposure Ladder step.
- Your child understands what he is expected to do to receive a reward.
- Your child has mastered the skills required to complete the step through rehearsal and role play.
- Necessary environmental adaptations are in place.
- A Worry Thermometer is ready for your child to rate their anxiety during the exposure step.
- You know which emotion management strategies you will use to keep yourself calm.

While Completing the Step

Complete the Exposure Ladder step by:

- Monitoring your child's anxiety by observing him and asking him to rate his anxiety on the Worry Thermometer. Keep in mind that you should expect to see his anxiety increase in the situation at first; however, it will then decrease.
- Encouraging your child to stay in the situation (if relevant) until he is no longer showing signs of anxiety. This may not always be possible, but his anxiety must reduce by at least half before he leaves the situation (otherwise, he is avoiding the situation via escape and thus increasing his anxiety).

Or:

- Encourage your child to complete the task.
- If needed, prompt your child to use his Emotional Toolbox strategies (discussed in later stages).
- Use praise to encourage your child to stay in the situation and to use emotion management strategies (e.g. 'You are making a brave choice by staying here! Great job using your deep breathing').
- Use your own emotion management strategies to keep calm.

After Completing the Step

After completing the Exposure Ladder step, it is important to remember the following:

- Immediately give your child lots of praise and his reward. Your child should receive a reward each time she tries hard to complete a step. Steps will never go perfectly but that is OK; if your child has tried her hardest, give her the reward.
- Sometimes you will attempt a step and things will not go to plan. If this happens, you and your child should focus on what she did well. In these instances, your child should still be praised and rewarded for what she did well. Your child may not receive the reward you agreed on, but she can be praised or rewarded with something smaller.
- Remember to keep a written record of your child's practice and her anxiety levels, so you can keep track of her progress. It is best to do this straight after your child completes a step.

Summary

Key points to remember when planning and implementing the Exposure Ladder with your child include:

- ✓ Your child needs to complete their Exposure Ladder step by staying in a situation until her anxiety significantly reduces (this usually takes 20–30 minutes).
- ✓ If your child fears a task (rather than a situation they can stay in), she needs to repeatedly complete her Exposure Ladder step (i.e. part of the task) until she experiences no or very minimal anxiety about completing this part of the task.
- ✓ Keep practising each step until your child experiences no or very minimal anxiety about the step.
- ✓ Ensure your child understands what is expected of her and what her reward will be.
- ✓ Monitor your child's anxiety throughout the step with the Anxiety Thermometer.
- ✓ Reward your child immediately after she has completed the step.

Weekly Plan Stage 4

To create and implement an Exposure Ladder with my child.

Action

Create an Exposure Ladder by following these steps:

Plan: Create an Exposure Ladder for Your Child

- ☐ Select a SMART goal.
- ☐ Make a list of small steps.
- ☐ Identify the skills your child will need to complete each step.
- ☐ Identify the environmental adaptations your child will need to complete each step.
- ☐ Put the steps in order of difficulty.
- ☐ Negotiate rewards.

My child's Exposure Ladder

Step	Difficulty/level of anxiety	Skills required/ environmental adaptations needed	Reward
1			
2			
3			
4			
5			
6			
7			
8			
9			

Happiness

Overview of Stage 5

The first aim of Stage 5 of *Fun with Feelings* is to help you understand some final reasons why children with ASD experience high levels of anxiety and why this anxiety does not decrease over time. In Stage 5 you will also start learning about the Toolbox that we will help you develop for your child, the Emotional Toolbox. The Emotional Toolbox includes a number of excellent tools that will assist your child throughout her life. In this stage we start with Awareness Tools. Awareness Tools are activities and strategies that you can use to teach your child about her emotions. This week you will learn how to use Awareness Tools to teach your child about the emotion *happiness*.

During Stage 5 you will learn:

- ✓ More reasons young children with ASD experience anxiety.
- ✓ The concept of the Emotional Toolbox for reducing anxiety.
- ✓ What Awareness Tools are and how to use them.
- ✓ How to start *Fun with Feelings* with your child using the activity booklets, including tips for creating a fun and successful experience for you and your child.
- ✓ Activities for teaching your child Awareness Tools to discover happiness including:
    - happiness and the different intensities at which happiness can be felt
    - other people's perspectives, thoughts and feelings
    - how to identify happiness in others
    - how to recognize internal body signs that indicate to us that we are happy.
- ✓ The Weekly Plan.

You will need:

- ✓ Your monitoring sheets from Stage 4.
- ✓ Happy Henry the Honeydew cut-out-and-colour-in puppet or a store-bought honeydew puppet.
- ✓ Scissors and glue.
- ✓ Coloured pencils or pens.
- ✓ Books, magazines or photographs of people with happy facial expressions.
- ✓ The Happiness Activity Booklet.
- ✓ This book.

Reflect on Weekly Plan Stage 4

In Stage 4 you started to create an Exposure Ladder to assist your child to gradually face one of their fears through small, manageable steps. You also brainstormed rewards to use to motivate your child to complete each step of the ladder. Last week, in the Weekly Plan, we asked you to finish creating this Exposure Ladder and to prepare all the materials you need to start using it.

Thinking about the Exposure Ladder you have created, do you have everything you need to start practising the first step on this ladder? What preparations have you undertaken?

What do you still need to prepare to be ready to practise the first step on the Exposure Ladder? For example, do you still need to organize rewards or Environmental Tools, or do you need to role-play skills with your child?

Congratulations on both completing Stage 4 and reflecting on your learning! You are on your way to achieving your goal!

More Reasons Children with ASD Experience High Levels of Anxiety

Let's examine some final reasons why anxiety may become a problem and stay a problem in young children with ASD.

Difficulties Understanding and Expressing Emotion

Children with ASD often have difficulty recognizing, interpreting and verbalizing their emotions. Children who have difficulty understanding and expressing emotions may:

- find it difficult to identify an emotion unless it is at an extreme or very high level
- find it difficult to separate themselves from their emotions and therefore may not feel in control of their emotions

- express emotions in a way that lacks subtlety and precision – for example, they may say 'I feel bad' or 'I don't like it' when, really, they are feeling a high level of anxiety
- have reactions that appear 'over the top' or 'too big' for the situation.

Because of these difficulties recognizing, interpreting and verbalizing emotions, often children with ASD do not attempt to regulate their emotions or get help to regulate their emotions until these emotions reach very high levels. However, it is very difficult for a child who is experiencing a high level of emotion to calm themselves down. Therefore, children with ASD often feel that their emotions are out of their control and that their attempts to control their emotions are unsuccessful. Equally, as you have probably experienced, it is very difficult to help a child in this state to calm down. Thus, children with ASD often miss out on learning effective emotion regulation skills and experience others' attempts to get them to use emotion regulation techniques as unhelpful. Further, even if emotion regulation strategies are effective in calming a child somewhat, because he (1) cannot easily identify changes in emotions, (2) believes his emotions are out of his control and (3) believes emotion regulation strategies are unhelpful, he may not learn the connection between emotion regulation strategies and feeling calmer.

Emotional Toolbox

The child's Emotional Toolbox contains tools that can be used by children with ASD, with the assistance of a parent or another adult, to decrease anxiety. There are six tools in the Emotional Toolbox:

- ✓ Awareness Tools
- ✓ Happy Tools
- ✓ Thought Tools
- ✓ Relaxation Tools
- ✓ Physical Tools
- ✓ Social Tools.

The final six stages (Stages 5–10) of *Fun with Feelings* focus on increasing your child's understanding of and ability to correctly identify emotions using Awareness Tools. Stages 5–10 of *Fun with Feelings* will also focus on increasing your child's ability to manage her feelings of anxiety using Happy Tools, Thought Tools, Relaxation Tools, Physical Tools and Social Tools.

In each stage, you will learn activities that you can use to teach your child about each tool as well as information on how to best practise the tools, model use of the tools and, finally, assist your child to use the tools when she is anxious.

Awareness Tools

Awareness Tools include a range of activities to complete with your child regularly to increase his understanding of and ability to correctly identify his emotions. Each tool in the Emotional Toolbox can assist your child to decrease his anxiety, but the tools will be most effective before your child experiences high or extreme levels of anxiety. Therefore, it is essential that your child first learns:

- how to identify when he is experiencing an emotion
- how to identify at what intensity he is experiencing an emotion
- how to differentiate between emotions
- when to use each tool in the Emotional Toolbox: Happy Tools, Thought Tools, Relaxation Tools, Physical Tools and Social Tools

We use Awareness Tools to achieve this learning. In each of Stages 5–10 we have provided you with an activity booklet to complete with your child. Each of these booklets includes activities you can use to teach your child about the emotions:

- Happiness
- Sadness
- Anxiety
- Relaxation
- Anger
- Affection.

To assist with this learning, we have also provided you with a set of cut-out-and-colour-in finger puppets. These add character to the emotion, which in turn makes the emotion more understandable for children. Your set of puppets contains six puppets:

- Happy Henry the Honeydew
- Sad Sally the Strawberry
- Worried Wanda the Watermelon
- Relaxed Ryan the Raspberry
- Angry Alan the Apple
- Loving Lulu the Lemon.

Over the next six stages you will learn how to complete the activities contained in each of the activity booklets with your child. There are also tips for making each of the activities a successful and fun experience for you and your child. Each activity booklet focuses on one emotion and contains Awareness Tools aimed at:

- introducing the emotion and meeting the corresponding puppet
- exploring the different levels of the emotion with a Feelings Thermometer
- understanding how different people experience the emotion
- understanding the body signs associated with the emotion
- identifying the emotion in others.

In addition to Awareness Tools, each of Stages 5–10 will also include activities for teaching your child how to use one of the other Emotional Tools which regulate emotions (i.e. Happy Tools, Thought Tools, Relaxation Tools, Physical Tools and Social Tools).

Making the Activity Booklets a Success

Most parents report that both they and their child enjoy completing the booklets together; however, as with any activity, challenges can arise while completing the booklets. Below are some key points to keep in mind when using the activity booklets:

- ✓ Complete the booklet at a time when your child is settled (preferably in the morning).

✓ Complete the booklet at a time when you are both feeling calm.
✓ Choose a place to complete the booklet that contains minimal distractions.
✓ Keep it short – only spend 2–10 minutes engaging in an activity at one time.
✓ Get down on your child's level.
✓ Be curious and open.
✓ Praise your child for any attempt (e.g. 'I love what you just said!', 'You are good at this!', 'That was a smart answer!', 'You are teaching me here!', 'I am having fun!', 'You are fun to be with!').
✓ Make it fun by taking a light-hearted approach.
✓ Be prepared to stop before the activity is finished and when your child is ready (i.e. stop at the first sign of your child showing tiredness or that they have had enough).
✓ Consider a reward system for any attempt made if your child is resistant to participating in the activities.

Introducing Happy Henry the Honeydew

We will start learning about emotions with Happy Henry the Honeydew. Happiness is a great emotion to teach first because while some children may feel defensive when discussing worry or anger, most children will not feel threatened by discussing happiness. Discussing what makes your child happy can be a rewarding experience for both of you.

The following information and activities aim to prepare you for teaching your child about the emotion happiness.

Happy Henry the Honeydew is the character that will be used to introduce happiness to your child. As we mentioned earlier, characters or puppets help to engage children and make emotions more understandable. In Appendix B there is a cut-out-and-colour-in Happy Henry the Honeydew finger puppet. On the first page of the Happiness Activity Booklet, there is a picture of Happy Henry and a short paragraph in which Happy Henry introduces herself. The paragraph reads:

Hi, I'm Happy Henry the Honeydew and I feel happy! When I'm happy, my eyes light up and my mouth has a great big smile, and sometimes I laugh. Being happy makes me feel so good inside. My body feels bouncy and full of energy! I feel happy playing with my friend or my favourite toy. I feel happy when I eat my favourite food, yoghurt. I feel happy when I go for a walk by the beach because it is fun! I like feeling happy. Seeing me happy makes other people feel happy too!

If your child can use scissors and colouring pencils, plan to cut out Happy Henry together and colour her in. If this task would be frustrating for your child or she would not enjoy it, cut out and colour in Happy Henry before you introduce her. Alternatively, use a honeydew puppet from a store.

Next, read Happy Henry's introduction to your child, using the finger puppet to act it out. Go ahead and be creative with this. Give Happy Henry a happy voice. Compare what makes her happy to what makes you and your child happy. Involve your child. Encourage him to make up a voice for Happy Henry, and to think of the activities and ideas that make him happy. Encourage your child to ask Happy Henry what makes her happy, and to enact Happy Henry asking your child what makes him happy.

Top Tip

Remember to match your child. If your child wants Happy Henry to be silly, then be silly! Children love to be silly, and they especially love it when grown-ups are silly. But if your child wants Happy Henry to be serious, then be serious. We can also be happy and serious at the same time.

Introducing the Emotional Toolbox

The next activity is to enact Happy Henry introducing the Emotional Toolbox. In your activity booklet there is a picture of Happy Henry saying:

Just as people need tools to fix things like broken toys and dripping taps, we all need tools for dealing with some feelings, such as too much anger, sadness or worry. Today I have told you some of my Happy Tools, like being on the beach and playing with my favourite toys. Happy Tools are the things that make you feel happy. I would love to know your Happy Tools!

Show your child this page and read the text in the speech bubble. Explore the idea of the toolbox with your child. See what tools they know – for example, a hammer, a paintbrush, a drill. Next, tell your child that they will be having fun with feelings by exploring the best tools they have for dealing with difficult feelings.

Turn to the next page in your booklet. On this page Happy Henry describes the Emotional Toolbox and Awareness Tools to your child. Read the text box to your child and discuss what this means. Your child may have many questions.

There are lots of types of tools in a normal toolbox. There are also lots of types of tools in your Emotional Toolbox. One of the most important tools in there is called an Awareness Tool. Awareness means knowing. Your Awareness Tools include knowing that you have feelings, knowing what they look like and feel like, and even knowing that you have tools that can help! Awareness Tools are some of our most powerful ones – they are the power tools in our toolbox, like the electrical drill. To deal with a feeling, you have to know it is there! And you cannot use a tool that you didn't know you had! Knowledge is very powerful. Together we are going to become very smart about you, your feelings and your tools.

Exploring Happiness Using a Feelings Thermometer

You will be using a thermometer to illustrate that emotions can be felt at different levels at different times. We can all experience low levels of an emotion such as annoyed (a low-level angry feeling) or glad (a low-level happy feeling), as well as high levels of emotions such as enraged (a high-level angry feeling) or ecstatic (a high-level happy feeling). Rating feelings on an Feelings Thermometer helps children to understand that emotions have differing levels of intensities, and to learn to recognize their own differing levels of emotions.

On page 9 of the Happiness Activity Booklet there is a picture of a Happy Thermometer with 'a little happy', 'happy' and 'really happy' levels. After this, there are three pages representing 'a little happy', 'happy' and 'really happy'. Finally, there is a page with pictures of activities and experiences that often elicit feelings of happiness in young children. These can be cut out and glued on to the Happy Thermometer.

Enact Happy Henry telling your child that she would like to know more about your child's happiness, including when he feels 'a little happy', 'happy' and 'really happy'. Act out Happy Henry asking your child how happy each of the suggested activities and experiences in the pictures makes him feel. Then help your child to cut out the happiness pictures and glue these on to the corresponding happiness level. After your child has glued on the happy pictures, encourage him to write or draw more of his happy activities and experiences on the corresponding section of the Happy Thermometer. Throughout the activity, also discuss with your child what makes you feel 'a little happy', 'happy' and 'really happy'.

Activity: Preparing for the Happy Thermometer Activity

First, note your own ideas for what makes your child 'a little happy', 'happy' and 'really happy'. These may fall into the categories of:

- activities
- sensory experiences (e.g. certain sounds, smells, tastes, colours or other visual experiences, tactile sensations)
- experiences
- memories
- books, movies and games
- compliments
- places
- people.

Next, write down your own ideas for what makes you happy across each of the three levels of happiness and consider what you feel comfortable sharing from your list with your child.

Collect images from the internet, magazines and your own photographs that correspond to the activities, memories, games and experiences that make your child feel happy.

Now you are ready to engage your child in this activity. Show him the images you have collected to represent happiness at various levels. Help him decide which images represent activities and experiences that make him happy. He may be able to cut out some pictures from magazines or choose pictures and photographs you are happy for him to use. Help him stick the pictures he has chosen into the Happiness Activity Booklet on the pages corresponding to the different levels of happiness – 'a little happy', 'happy' and 'really happy'.

Exploring Other People's Perspectives Through the 'We Are All Different' Activity

The next activity in your child's activity booklet is called 'We Are All Different'. We know that young children with ASD often struggle with Theory of Mind – that is, they often struggle to understand that other people have thoughts, feelings, desires and beliefs that are different to their own. The 'We Are All Different' Activity is designed to help your child to learn that sometimes other people have the same thoughts and feelings as she does, but sometimes others have thoughts and feelings that are different to her own.

On page 14 of the Happiness Activity Booklet there is space for you or your child to write:

- one thing that makes you and your child happy
- one thing that makes your child happy but does not make you happy
- one thing that makes you happy but does not make your child happy.

Read through each of these questions with your child, discuss potential answers, then write these answers in the booklet.

Activity: Preparing for the 'We Are All Different' Activity

It is helpful to have some suggestions ready for potential answers in the 'We Are All Different' Activity.

What makes you and your child happy?

What makes your child happy but does not make you happy?

What makes you happy but does not make your child happy?

Top Tip

Remember, when having this discussion with your child, there are basically no wrong answers. The idea is to validate and accept that we are all different. However, a small number of answers are unacceptable. An example of such an unacceptable answer is an antisocial one – for example, hitting or hurting other people. If your child nominates answers such as these, it can be an indication of underlying anger or rage towards that person, or generalized anger. It can be helpful to validate that sometimes we feel angry with people, and feel like hurting them, but that usually these feelings pass and later we can feel very unhappy if we did hurt someone while we were angry. Move on to discuss other ideas and experiences that cause happiness. It can be helpful to include Happy Henry in the discussions, particularly if your child seems to enjoy speaking to Happy Henry.

Learning to Identify Happiness in Others Through the 'Mr Face' Activity

The 'Mr Face' Activity aims to increase your child's understanding of and ability to recognize a happy facial expression. Children with ASD often have difficulty making facial expressions and recognizing facial expressions in others, so although this activity may seem basic, it is likely to be new knowledge for your child, and a wonderful foundation stone for him to start thinking about and understanding his own and other people's emotions.

On page 15 of the Happiness Activity Booklet there is a picture of a blank face. You will also need some pictures from the internet and magazines with pictures of happy faces. It may be helpful to have photographs of your child and people he likes and loves showing happy facial expressions.

Begin the 'Mr Face' Activity by showing your child the pictures and photographs of happy faces. Ask your child to point out what makes these faces happy. He is very likely first to point out the mouth. Praise him for this correct answer. Then ask if there are other aspects of the face that look happy. If your child does not point to the eyes, point these out to him. Research shows that children with ASD tend not to look at the eyes for information about what a person may be thinking or feeling. Therefore, teaching your child to orient his gaze towards other people's eyes will help him to learn how to read other people and thus develop more attuned perspective-taking skills.

You can further this learning by asking your child to look at your face while you are smiling and to guess when the happiness reaches your eyes. You can also cover your mouth and nose so your child can only see your eyes and ask him to guess when the happiness reaches your eyes. Of course, it is important during this exercise that you keep your eyes neutral or blank until a certain point and then decide to bring happiness into them.

When your child seems to really understand what makes a happy face, ask him to make one for you. You can also suggest to your child that he makes a happy face in the mirror, or makes a video or photograph of his happy face. Next, ask him to draw a happy face in his activity booklet.

Exploring Happy Body Signs Through the 'Happy Body, Happy Mind' Activity

We will be using guided imagery to help your child to better understand and recognize her feelings of happiness. All emotions, including happiness, can be felt in the body. Therefore, learning to identify and interpret physiological signs of emotions will improve your child's ability to understand, recognize and vocalize her emotions. We recommend doing the 'Happy Body, Happy Mind' Activity first yourself and notice your own bodily sensations as you start to feel happy. Being able to experience a 'felt sense' of your own happiness will help you to know what your child is looking for when she practises this exercise.

For the 'Happy Body, Happy Mind' Activity, ask your child to sit or lie in her favourite spot in the house and to vividly imagine her own favourite activity, or an experience that brings her a high level of happiness. Once your child is deeply experiencing an imaginal version of a happy time, ask her to tune in to her body and to notice what is happening in her body right at that moment while she is experiencing happiness. To assist you with this task we have included in her activity booklet a script to read to your child to guide her through imagining happiness.

Some children with ASD can find this exercise difficult. They may not intuitively know how to 'tune in' to their own bodily sensations. In other words, their ability to detect sensations (e.g. tense muscles, a knot in the stomach, a rush of energy) going on in their own body is not yet developed. Other children with ASD may detect their bodily sensations but find it difficult to explain these sensations with words. Our suggestion is to allow time for your child to experience the feelings. It may work best to ask her to continue to imagine the happy time while experiencing her body, with no requirement to describe these body sensations until after the imaginal exercise. If your child has difficulty describing what is going on in her body while she is happy, she may be able to draw it using shapes or colour later. If you have completed this activity yourself, you can share what you discovered about your own bodily sensations of happiness. Your child may well respond to some of the following descriptions from typically developing children:

- I feel tingling and alive.
- I feel light and buzzing.
- Light in my body.
- Energizing, feel like jumping up and down, flapping my arms or hands.
- Soft feelings in my arms, legs, tummy.
- Good; my body feels good.
- My tummy feels warm.

Weekly Plan Stage 5

The first goal for this week's Weekly Plan is to start using Awareness Tools to teach your child about emotions, starting with happiness, including how happiness feels in her body, the various levels of happiness she experiences, how to recognize happiness in faces and to understand that people differ in what makes them happy. Following on from the 'We Are All Different' Activity, we ask you to start noticing when you are feeling happy and sharing these feelings with your child, including how you noticed happiness in your body.

The second goal for Stage 5 is to implement Step 1 of the Exposure Ladder that you created last week.

Actions to Start Exploring Happiness and Increasing Awareness

Your Weekly Plan involves preparing for, scheduling and then completing the following activities with your child:

1. Meeting Happy Henry
2. Exploring different levels of happiness with a Happy Thermometer
3. We Are All Different
4. Mr Face
5. Happy Body, Happy Mind.

Using the Weekly Plan, pencil in times to complete activities in the Happiness Activity Booklet with your child this week (Activities 1–5). Remember, it is important to complete the booklet via several small learning sessions rather than one long learning session. Then, over the next week, at these scheduled times, complete each of the five tasks in the activity booklet with your child.

Throughout the week, notice when you are feeling happy. Tell your child that you are feeling happy at these times as well as the level of your happiness on your thermometer. If he is not there at the time, ensure that you tell him at a later time – for example, during conversation at dinner or during the bedtime routine. When you describe what made you feel happy, also describe in simple terms how your body felt when you were happy. Telling our children about how our emotions feel is one of the best ways that we can increase their emotional intelligence and assist them with their own emotion regulation.

Top Tip

Make a commitment to be kind to yourself and your child. You have probably never completed something like this with your child before – you are both trying something new. As much as you can, make room in your mind for learning. This means allowing for the possibility for each of you to try, fail, try, succeed, try again, fail, try and so on.

FAQs – Exploring Happiness and Increasing Awareness

What if I never feel happy?
There can be times in our lives where we feel that we never experience happiness. Even when we remember past happy times, this can just make us sad as those times are over and we feel we will never be happy again. If this is your experience, it is very important to acknowledge this and to decide to do something about it. Such thinking is very characteristic of depression, and depression is very common among family members of those with ASD because of the genetic link between ASD and depression. The good news is that depression is treatable. If you are really struggling to remember experiences and activities that make you feel happy, do make an appointment to see your GP or a clinical psychologist for an assessment to determine whether you are experiencing clinical depression. If you are, commit to getting better as your primary goal to assist your child.

What if I cannot tell if my child feels happy and she cannot tell me when she feels happy?
Sometimes children with ASD can be very difficult to read because they show few facial expressions. Also, because of difficulties formulating their thoughts and feelings into words, they may not tell us how they feel. If this is the case for your child, we recommend observing closely the activities that she spends considerable time on or activities that calm her down. It is these activities that are likely to be associated with happiness, even if your child cannot tell you that this is true.

What if the only activities that my child enjoys are ones that I want him to reduce (e.g. computer games)?
It is important that we do not discount the happiness activities bring our children even if we wish they would engage in these activities less, as long

as these activities do not harm them or others. Validating our children's emotions, including happiness, is very important for assisting them to understand when they have these emotions, and to understand that taking notice of these emotions is important.

**What if my child just does not want to engage
in any conversations about feelings?**

Although this is uncommon, it does happen. Usually the reasons behind the child's resistance are perfectionism, a fear of making a mistake and a need to be right. The child perceives that this is a topic that she struggles with, and she does not want to be revealed as someone who does not know or to appear stupid. If this is the case, we recommend acknowledging that it can be difficult to approach a new topic that we have not thought about very much. Tell your child that even some adults do not talk about their feelings very much, and that it is perfectly normal not to want to. Nevertheless, explain that it is an important topic and one that she will need to know about throughout her whole life. Explain that one of your roles (jobs) in her life is as a teacher, and you would not be doing your job properly if you didn't teach her the vital information she needs to know about emotions. Explain that the whole day will not be filled with talking about feelings, that discussions will be brief, and that after each discussion about feelings, the child can choose a topic she wants to talk about. If you use this strategy, ensure that you consistently reward the child for any discussion about feelings with a discussion about her own chosen topic for at least the same amount of time as the 'feelings' conversation has taken.

Actions to Start Implementing the Exposure Ladder with Your Child

Refresh your memory about Step 1 of your Exposure Ladder. Using the Weekly Plan, pencil times that may be good times to practise Step 1. Prior to commencing the step, practise the skills needed to complete each step and explain both the step and the reward to your child.

We recommend that you aim to practise this first step 3–4 times this week. Below is a checklist to assist you to implement Step 1. We recommend you use this checklist each time you practise Step 1; then complete the Exposure Ladder Practice Monitoring Form after each time.

Checklist to Climb the Exposure Ladder with Your Child

- ☐ Attempt the step.
- ☐ Monitor your child's anxiety before, during and after the step.
- ☐ Encourage your child to use a tool from their Emotional Toolbox.
- ☐ Reward your child.
- ☐ Record your child's practice and anxiety levels.

FAQs – Practising Step 1 of the Exposure Ladder

What if my child refuses to practise a step?
If your child refuses to complete a step, do not give him a reward. Instead, try again another day. If your child continues to refuse to practise a step, ask yourself:

- Is the reward motivating enough?
- Is this step too difficult for my child right now?
- Can I make this step easier?

What if my child says he is too sick to practise?
Feeling sick in the stomach is a common physiological sign of anxiety. If your child feels sick when practising a step, encourage him to use his relaxation strategies to help bring the anxiety under control. The sick feeling will decrease as your child's anxiety decreases.

How many times will my child need to practise each step?
There is no set number of times your child will need to practise a step. Keep practising a step until your child no longer shows signs of anxiety while completing the step.

When should my child not receive a reward?
Don't give your child a reward if he refuses to practise or runs away during practice. If you give your child a reward at these times, you will accidentally reinforce his anxious behaviour.

Exposure Ladder Practice Monitoring Form

Day	Exposure Ladder step practised	Successfully practised (i.e. your child remained in the situation until their anxiety decreased) Y/N	Comments
1			
2			
3			
4			
5			
6			
7			

Sadness and Happy Tools

Overview of Stage 6

The aim of Stage 6 is to introduce activities that you can use to teach your child about the emotion *sadness*. You will also learn about another set of tools from the Emotional Toolbox. The new set of tools introduced in this stage are Happy Tools.

During Stage 6 you will learn:

- ✓ Sadness Awareness Tools:
    - Activities you can use to teach your child about the emotion sadness and the different intensities sadness can be felt
    - Activities you can use to teach your child about other people's perspectives, thoughts and feelings
    - Activities you can use to teach your child to identify sadness in others
    - Activities you can use to teach your child about how sadness feels in the body.
- ✓ Happy Tools:
    - Activities you can use to teach your child how to use Happy Tools.
- ✓ Tips for practising Happy Tools.
- ✓ Tips for modelling using Happy Tools.
- ✓ The Weekly Plan.

You will need:

- ✓ Your monitoring sheets from Stage 5.
- ✓ Sad Sally the Strawberry cut-out-and-colour-in puppet or a store-bought strawberry puppet.
- ✓ Scissors and glue.
- ✓ Colouring pencils and pens.
- ✓ Books, magazines or photographs of people showing sad facial expressions.
- ✓ The Sadness Activity Booklet.
- ✓ This book.

Reflect on Weekly Plan Stage 5

In Stage 5 we asked you to complete the Happiness Activity Booklet and to practise the first step on your child's Exposure Ladder.

Completing the Happiness Activity Booklet

What went well? What activities did your child enjoy? What new concepts did your child understand?

What did not go well? What barriers did you face – for example, not enough time, not enough support, not enough knowledge, not enough confidence?

Considering your experience and your reflection and all that you now know, what did you learn from the task?

After reflecting on the successes and difficulties you experienced completing the Happiness Activity Booklet with your child, would you change anything before completing the Sadness Activity Booklet with your child?

Practising the First Step on the Exposure Ladder

Did your child master this step? Is your child ready to move on to the next step on their Exposure Ladder? Remember, your child has mastered their current step and is ready to move on to their next step once their anxiety has reduced significantly (i.e. reduced by at least 50%).

What challenges did you face before, during and after practising the Exposure Ladder step with your child?

After reflecting on the successes and difficulties you experienced practising the Exposure Ladder step, would you change anything before practising the next step with your child?

Top Tip

To assist with overcoming challenges for completing the Happiness Activity Booklet with your child, check back to page 134, "Making the Activity Booklets a Success." To assist you to overcome any challenges in implementing the exposure hierarchy, reread the sections starting on page 124 with "Before you Complete an Exposure Ladder Step."

Introducing Sad Sally the Strawberry

Sad Sally the Strawberry is the character that will be used to introduce sadness to your child. In Appendix B there is a cut-out-and-colour-in Sad Sally the Strawberry finger puppet. On the first page of the Sadness Activity Booklet, there is a picture of Sad Sally and a short paragraph in which Sad Sally introduces herself. This paragraph reads:

Hi, I'm Sad Sally the Strawberry and I feel sad. When I'm sad, my eyes look down, my face has a frown and sometimes I cry. Being sad makes my body feel heavy and droopy. I feel sad when my toy breaks or someone is mean to me or won't let me play. I feel sad when someone I care about goes away. I feel sad when my mum and dad won't let me do something I want to do. Feeling sad isn't a very nice feeling.

If your child can use scissors and colouring pencils, plan to cut out Sad Sally together and colour her in. If this task would be frustrating for your child or he would not enjoy it, cut out and colour in Sad Sally before you introduce her. Alternatively, use a strawberry puppet from a store.

Then read through the introduction with your child, using the finger puppet to act it out. Give Sad Sally her own unique voice and compare what makes her sad with what makes you and your child sad.

Ideas for discussing Sad Sally the Strawberry:

- ✓ Use a slow and quiet voice for Sad Sally.
- ✓ Have Sad Sally cry when talking about things that make her really sad.
- ✓ Make Sad Sally's movements heavy and slow.
- ✓ Encourage your child to do or say something to help Sad Sally feel less sad.
- ✓ Ensure that, as Sad Sally, you ask your child questions about what makes him sad and you listen to his answers.
- ✓ Follow your child's lead. If your child is having difficulty talking about what makes him sad and just wants to talk about Sad Sally, then allow him to do so.

Exploring Sadness Using a Feelings Thermometer

A Feelings Thermometer will be used to facilitate discussion of what makes your child 'a little sad', 'sad' and 'really sad'.

Using Sad Sally's voice, act out Sad Sally telling your child that she would like to know more about your child's sadness, including what makes him 'a little sad', 'sad' and 'really sad'. Then help your child to cut out and stick each sad picture on the thermometer level where your child thinks it should go. After your child has stuck on the sad pictures, encourage him to draw or write more of his sad triggers on the corresponding 'a little sad', 'sad' and 'really sad' pages. Throughout the activity also discuss with your child what makes you sad.

Many young children do not have much experience with feeling sad and will only be able to name a few experiences of feeling sad. This is fine.

Activity: Preparing for the Sad Thermometer Activity

It is important for you to have a few suggestions up your sleeve to contribute if necessary. Below, write down ideas for what makes your child 'a little sad', 'sad' and 'really sad'.

Next, write down your own ideas for what makes you sad across each of the three levels of sad and consider what you feel comfortable sharing from your list with your child.

Exploring Other People's Perspectives Through the 'We Are All Different' Activity

The next activity in your child's Sadness Activity Booklet is called 'We Are All Different'. The 'We Are All Different' Activity is designed to help your child to learn that sometimes other people have the same thoughts and feelings as she does, but sometimes others have thoughts and feelings that are different to her own.

On page 26 of the Sadness Activity Booklet there is space for you or your child to write:

- one thing that makes you and your child sad
- one thing that makes your child sad but does not make you sad
- one thing that makes you sad but does not make your child sad.

Read through each of these questions with your child, discuss potential answers, then write these answers in the booklet.

Activity: Preparing for the 'We Are All Different' Activity

It is helpful to have some suggestions ready for potential answers in the 'We Are All Different' Activity.

What makes you and your child sad?

What makes your child sad but does not make you sad?

What makes you sad but does not make your child sad?

Learning to Identify Facial Expression Through the 'Mr Face' Activity

The next activity in the Sadness Activity Booklet is the 'Mr Face' Activity. This activity aims to further help your child think about and understand his own and other people's emotions.

On page 27 of the Sadness Activity Booklet there is a picture of a blank face. You will also need some pencils and some books and magazines with pictures of sad faces. It can also be helpful to have some photographs of your child and people he loves showing sad faces.

Begin the activity by showing your child pictures and photographs of sad faces. Ask your child to point out what makes these faces sad. Point out to your child that a sad face has:

- eyes looking down
- low eyebrows
- corners of the mouth turned down.

Then, when your child understands what makes a sad face, ask him to make one for you, or to make a sad face in the mirror, or to make a video or photograph. Next, ask your child to draw a sad face in his Sadness Activity Booklet. Remember to give your child praise and encouragement at each step in this activity.

Exploring Sad Body Signs Through the 'Sad Body, Sad Mind' Activity

As with the emotion happiness, we will be using guided imagery to help your child to better understand and recognize her feelings of sadness. All emotions, including sadness, can be felt in the body. Thus, learning to identify and interpret physiological signs of emotions will improve your child's ability to understand, recognize and vocalize her emotions.

For the 'Sad Body, Sad Mind' Activity, ask your child to sit or lie in her favourite spot in the house and to vividly imagine a time when she felt sad. Your child may need your assistance to remember such a time, so it can be helpful to think of a specific time when your child felt sad before the activity (e.g. a time when your child was sick, lost a special toy, watched a sad scene in a movie). Once your child is deeply experiencing an imaginal version of a sad time, ask her to tune in to her body and to notice what is happening in her body right at that moment while she is experiencing sadness. To assist you with this task we have included a script to read to your child to guide her through imagining sadness. The script is in the Sadness Activity Booklet.

Some children with ASD can find this exercise difficult. If your child has difficulty describing what is going on in her body while she is sad, she may be able to draw it using shapes or colour later. Or she may respond to some of the following descriptions from typically developing children:

- I feel heavy.
- My body is trembling.
- Dark in my body.
- No energy, I want to lie down.
- Heavy feelings in my arms, legs, tummy.
- Cold, my body feels cold.
- My heart feels empty.

Happy Tools from the Emotions Toolbox

In addition to increasing your child's understanding of and ability to correctly identify emotions using Awareness Tools and starting to think about Happy Tools, Stages 6–10 of the programme will also focus on increasing your child's ability to manage his emotions using emotion regulation strategies. The second half of each activity booklet in Stages 6–10 will contain activities designed to teach your child about one of the five remaining tools from the Emotional Toolbox: Happy Tools, Thought Tools, Relaxation Tools, Physical Tools and Social Tools. Stage 6 contains activities you can use to teach your child about Happy Tools. Happy Tools, as you will remember, are simply pleasurable activities that engage your child's attention. Engaging in a pleasurable activity is a very effective way to:

- decrease feelings of anxiety, anger or sadness
- increase feelings of happiness and relaxation
- restore energy.

Powerful Happy Tools for children with ASD are often activities that are:

- repetitive or highly predictable
- related to your child's special interest
- undertaken in solitude.

Because Happy Tools involve activities that are extremely effective at alleviating negative feelings, children can become obsessively fixated on completing these activities. This often occurs when a child has no other Emotional Tools that they can access to reduce negative feelings. Thus, although it is important for children to be able to access Happy Tools to help them regulate their emotions, it is also important that children learn other Emotional Tools and that time spent in pleasurable activities is kept to a reasonable time frame. Also, it is important that children are not encouraged to use Happy Tools as a way of avoiding a situation or task they are afraid of. As we have discussed in earlier stages, avoidance of feared situations or tasks simply strengthens anxiety. Instead, children should be encouraged to engage in Happy Tools at regular, scheduled times. For example, straight after school is a great time to encourage your child to engage in Happy Tools as a way of de-stressing from the busy school day and restoring energy.

Revisiting Happy Tools

On page 29 of the Sadness Activity Booklet, Sad Sally explains that when she is worried, sad or angry, she can use her Happy Tools to help her feel happy and relaxed again. Then, on the next pages, there are some suggestions for Happy Tools your child can try as well as space for your child to add his own ideas for Happy Tools.

To begin the activity, read through the introduction using the Happy Henry puppet to act it out. Then, on the next page, help your child to circle Happy Tools he would like to try and draw or write his own ideas of Happy Tools.

Activity: Preparing for the Happy Tools Activity

As always, it is important for you to have a few suggestions up your sleeve to contribute if necessary. Below, write down ideas for activities that capture your child's attention and make him feel happy or relaxed:

Practising Happy Tools

Your Weekly Plan this week includes scheduling time for your child to engage in at least one of her Happy Tools each day and helping your child to rate her feelings before and after using her Happy Tools. On page 31 of the Sadness Activity Booklet there is a table for your child to record her feelings before and after completing their Happy Tool. Some families find that removing this page from the activity booklet (or photocopying it) and sticking it on the fridge or a family notice board helps to remind them to complete this monitoring.

Unlike some of the other tools from the Emotional Toolbox, children do not need to learn how to use Happy Tools; however, it is important that they use these on a daily basis to reduce negative feelings and increase feelings of happiness and calm. It is also important that they learn to identify the effect Happy Tools can have on their emotions.

Using Happy Tools Yourself

It is important that you practise using Happy Tools yourself so that you can:

- ✓ have lower overall levels of stress, anxiety and depression
- ✓ more easily and confidently teach your child how to use the tools
- ✓ model effective emotion regulation to your child.

Activity for Parents: Scheduling Happy Tools

Take a moment to consider the activities that bring you happiness. Include small activities that you can use daily, as well as larger activities that you may need to plan to have time for. List these here:

Daily pleasurable activities	Longer pleasurable activities
Slowly sip a cup of your favourite tea in the sun or shade of a tree Imagine your favourite holiday	Meet friends for a coffee or a bike ride Read some of your book Go to the movies or a class

Modelling Use of Happy Tools

It is also important to model effective emotion regulation to your child by visibly using your own Happy Tools. You are your child's most powerful influence, whether you feel this to be so or not. In Stage 5 we asked you to share with your child when you were feeling happy, how happy you felt and why you felt happy. This week, as a part of the Weekly Plan, we ask you to notice when you are feeling stressed or tense and to model using a Happy Tool by saying a version of this script:

> I just noticed that I am beginning to feel a little sad. My body feels heavy and tense. I am going to use one of my Happy Tools and read a book.

Later, after using your Happy Tool, make a comment like this to your child:

> Aaah. I feel much better. My sadness is gone. Happy Tools are wonderful!

Adjust this script to suit your style and your child's level of understanding.

Weekly Plan Stage 6

The first goal for the Stage 6 Weekly Plan is to start teaching your child about the emotion sadness, including the various levels of sadness he experiences, how sadness feels in the body, how to recognize sad faces and that people differ in what makes them sad. The second goal for Stage 6 is to start teaching your child how to use Happy Tools. The third goal for Stage 6 is to practise the second step from your child's Exposure Ladder.

Your Weekly Plan involves preparing for, scheduling and then completing the following activities with your child:

1. Meeting Sad Sally
2. Exploring different levels of sadness with a Sad Thermometer
3. We Are All Different
4. Mr Face
5. Sad Body Signs
6. Happy Tools
7. Daily practice of Happy Tools

8. Modelling use of Happy Tools
9. Practising the Exposure Ladder step.

Action

Using the Weekly Plan, pencil in times that may be good times to complete the five 2–10 minute activities with your child this week (Activities 1–5). Then, over the next week, at these scheduled times, complete each of the six tasks in the Sadness Activity Booklet with your child.

Once you have completed the Sadness Activity Booklet, schedule 2–10 minutes each day to practise a Happy Tool with your child when she is already calm and/or happy. Use the self-monitoring sheet in the activity booklet to track your child's emotions and make any notes.

Throughout the week, try to notice times when you or your child are feeling sad. If you are sad, tell your child what level of sadness you are experiencing and what sad body signs you are experiencing. If your child appears sad, ask her to rate her level of sadness and to describe her sad body signs.

Throughout the week, also model using Happy Tools to improve your mood.

Using the Weekly Plan, select the second step from your child's Exposure Ladder and pencil in times that may be good times to practise this step. If your child did not master the first step on their Exposure Ladder, then practise this step again. If your child did master the first step on their Exposure Ladder, then move on to the next step. Over the next week, at these scheduled times, practise this step with your child. Finally, complete the Exposure Ladder Practice Monitoring Form.

Exposure Ladder Practice Monitoring Form

Day	Exposure Ladder step practised	Successfully practised (i.e. your child remained in the situation until their anxiety decreased) Y/N	Comments
1			
2			
3			
4			
5			
6			
7			

Worry and Thought Tools

Overview of Stage 7

The aim of Stage 7 is to introduce activities that you can use to teach your child about the emotion *worry*. You will also learn about another set of tools from the Emotional Toolbox, Thought Tools, and activities you can use to teach your child how to use Thought Tools.

During Stage 7 you will learn:

- ✓ Anxiety Awareness Tools:
    - – Activities you can use to teach your child about the emotion worry and the different intensities at which worry can be felt.
    - – Activities you can use to teach your child to recognize worry in others.
    - – Activities you can use to teach your child to recognize worry in himself, both in his body and his behaviour.
    - – Activities you can use to teach your child the difference between helpful worry (worry in response to dangerous situations) and unhelpful worry (worry in response to safe situations).
    - – Activities you can use to teach your child about other people's perspectives, thoughts and feelings.
- ✓ Thought Tools:
    - – Activities you can use to teach your child to use Thought Tools.
- ✓ Tips for practising using Thought Tools.
- ✓ Tips for modelling using Thought Tools.
- ✓ Tips for helping your child to use Thought Tools when he is anxious.
- ✓ The Weekly Plan.

You will need:

- ✓ Your monitoring sheets from Stage 6.
- ✓ Worried Wanda the Watermelon cut-out-and-colour-in puppet or a store-bought watermelon puppet.
- ✓ Scissors and glue.
- ✓ Colouring pencils and pens.
- ✓ Books, magazines or photographs of people showing worried facial expressions.
- ✓ The Worry Activity Booklet.
- ✓ This book.

Reflect on Weekly Plan Stage 6

In Stage 6, we asked you to complete the second step on your child's Exposure Ladder. We also asked you to complete the Sadness Activity Booklet with your child.

Completing the Sadness Activity Booklet
What went well?

What did not go well? What barriers/challenges did you face – for example, not enough time, not enough support, not enough knowledge, not enough confidence?

Considering your experience and your reflection and all that you now know, what did you learn from the task?

After reflecting on the successes and difficulties you experienced completing the Sadness Activity Booklet with your child, would you change anything before completing the Worry Activity Booklet with your child?

Happy Tools

What successes did you encounter when practising the Happy Tools with your child?

What challenges did you encounter when practising the Happy Tools with your child?

Practising a Step on the Exposure Ladder
Which Exposure Ladder step did you practise with your child?

Did your child master this step? Is your child ready to move on to the next step on their Exposure Ladder? Remember, your child has mastered their current step and is ready to move on to their next step once their anxiety has reduced significantly (i.e. reduced by at least 50%).

What have been the successes with the Exposure Ladder?

What are the challenges that arise when you are trying to complete the Exposure Ladder?

After reflecting on the successes and difficulties you experienced practising the Exposure Ladder step, would you change anything before practising the next step with your child?

Top Tip

To assist with overcoming challenges for completing the Sadness Activity Booklet with your child, check back to page 134, "Making the Activity Booklets a Success." To assist you to overcome any challenges in implementing the exposure hierarchy, reread the sections starting on page 124 with "Before you Complete an Exposure Ladder Step."

[AQ] Emotion Education about the Emotion Anxiety

Stage 7 of the programme focuses on increasing your child's understanding of and ability to recognize anxiety. As young children are often unfamiliar with the word 'anxiety', we use the more understandable and common word 'worry' to explain anxiety to children. If your child refers to their anxiety as nervousness or stress or any other word, please use this word instead when discussing worry with your child. As mentioned in earlier stages of the programme, young children with ASD often have difficulty identifying emotions and often do not identify a distressing emotion until it is at an extreme level. This is very problematic when managing anxiety because by the time your child has reached extreme levels of anxiety (or a meltdown), it is very difficult for them to calm down, even with the assistance of anxiety management strategies. The anxiety management strategies found in the Emotional Toolbox can assist your child to decrease any level of anxiety, but they will be most effective before your child experiences extreme levels of anxiety, so helping your child to learn to recognize the early signs is very important.

The following activities aim to prepare you for teaching your child about the emotion worry.

Introducing Worried Wanda the Watermelon

Worried Wanda the Watermelon is the character that will be used to introduce anxiety to your child. In Appendix B there is a cut-out-and-colour-in Worried Wanda the Watermelon finger puppet. On the first page of the Worry Activity Booklet there is a picture of Worried Wanda and a short paragraph in which Worried Wanda introduces herself. This paragraph reads:

Hi, I'm Worried Wanda the Watermelon and I feel worried. When I feel worried, my eyes go wide, my eyebrows go up, my lips start to shake and I put my hands on my face. When I feel worried, my stomach has butterflies, my hands get all sweaty and my legs become wobbly. I feel worried when someone I care about is sick and when I think I might get into trouble. I feel worried before I go on scary rides and if someone is mad at me. I do not like feeling worried.

As with the previous characters, if your child is happy to use scissors and colouring pencils, cut out Worried Wanda together and colour her in. Otherwise, cut out and colour in Worried Wanda yourself before you introduce her to your child or use a store-bought watermelon puppet. Once your child and/or you have created the Worried Wanda puppet, read through the introduction with your child, using the finger puppet to act out the emotion. Give Wanda her own unique voice or encourage your child to make up a voice for Wanda.

Ideas for discussing Worried Wanda the Watermelon:

- ✓ Use a shy quiet voice for Worried Wanda.
- ✓ Pretend that Worried Wanda is hiding and afraid to meet your child.
- ✓ Encourage your child to do or say something to help Worried Wanda feel less anxious.
- ✓ Ensure that, as Worried Wanda, you ask your child questions about what makes her worried and you listen to her answers.
- ✓ Follow your child's lead. If your child is having difficulties talking about her worries and just wants to talk about Worried Wanda's worries, then do so.

Exploring Worry Using a Feelings Thermometer

On the next page of the activity booklet is the Worry Thermometer activity. The Feelings Thermometer will again be used to facilitate discussion of what makes your child 'a little worried', 'worried' and 'really worried'. This may be a confronting emotion to discuss for some children, so take it gently. Using the finger puppet may help, and you can ask your child what makes Worried Wanda 'a little worried', 'worried' and 'really worried'. There are two helpful activities below to complete prior to this discussion. Completing these activities will assist you to be more aware of your child's triggers and behavioural signs of worry.

Using Worried Wanda's voice, act out Worried Wanda telling your child that she would like to know more about your child's worry, including when your child feels 'a little worried', 'worried' and 'really worried', and how he knows he is worried about something. During this discussion, write or draw your child's triggers and behavioural signs on the pages for this in the activity booklet. Throughout the activity also discuss with your child what makes you feel 'a little worried', 'worried' and 'really worried'.

Activity: Preparing for the Worry Thermometer Activity

In the spaces provided below, write down some of the triggers for your child's worry. This preparation will help you to work on the Worry Thermometer Activity with your child this week. It will be helpful for you to have a few suggestions up your sleeve to contribute if necessary.

Situations:

Places:

Tasks:

Sensory experiences (e.g. sounds, smells, tastes, colours or other visual experiences, and tactile sensations):

Experiences:

Movies or stories:

Next, place these triggers for anxiety on the Worry Thermometer to signify whether each makes your child 'a little worried', 'worried' or 'really worried'.

It will also be helpful for you to reflect on, and write down, your own triggers for what makes you feel worried across each of the three levels of worry, and then consider what you feel comfortable sharing from your list with your child.

Top Tip

Worried Wanda can join in the Thermometer Activity at any point to elaborate on the concept of worry, to validate worries or to discuss other people's worries.

Learning to Identify Behavioural Signs That Your Child Feels Anxiety or Worry

As described above, children with ASD often show that they are feeling anxious through their behaviour. To prepare for this activity, consider the following list of behaviours and tick any that apply to your child. Throughout this stage you will be drawing your child's attention to these behavioural signs that she is feeling worried and placing them on the 'Worry Thermometer' in her activity booklet:

- ☐ Repeatedly asking the same question but knowing the answer.
- ☐ Seeking reassurance that an event is going to happen.
- ☐ Lining up toys.
- ☐ Refusing to change to another activity.
- ☐ Fiddling with a sensory toy.
- ☐ Pacing.
- ☐ Insisting on the completion of a ritual.
- ☐ Talking incessantly about a previous event associated with worry.
- ☐ Rocking.
- ☐ Twiddling fingers.
- ☐ Being irritable.
- ☐ Trying to take control of events.
- ☐ Insisting on having access to technology or to engage in the special interest.
- ☐ Running away.
- ☐ Avoiding what he is worried about.
- ☐ 'Freezing' – i.e. becoming mute or very still.
- ☐ Other: _____ .

Exploring Other People's Perspectives Through the 'We Are All Different' Activity

The next activity in your child's activity booklet is called 'We Are All Different'. The 'We Are All Different' Activity is designed to help your child to learn that sometimes other people have the same thoughts and feelings as he does, but sometimes others have thoughts and feelings that are different to his own.

On page 39 of the Worry Activity Booklet there is space for you or your child to write:

- one thing that makes you and your child worried
- one thing that makes your child worried, but does not make you worried
- one thing that makes you worried, but does not make your child worried.

Read through each of these questions with your child, discuss potential answers, then write these answers in the booklet.

Activity: Preparing for the 'We Are All Different' Activity

It is helpful to have some suggestions ready for potential answers in the 'We Are All Different' Activity. It is important to include only the triggers for your own worry that are at a low level for you, so as not to accidentally share your worry with your child, and thus increase her worries. A low-level worry for a parent might include whether your child brushes her teeth or not. Most children already know that although this is a concern for their parent, it is not really worrying them. For this activity, it is important to remember that worry is very contagious!

What makes you and your child worried?

What makes your child worried but does not make you worried?

What makes you worried but does not make your child worried?

Learning to Identify Facial Expressions Through the 'Mr Face' Activity

The 'Mr Face' Activity involves asking your child to explore what a worried face looks like. This is a wonderful activity to help your child to start thinking about and understanding his own and other people's emotions. It is also helpful for your child to learn to reference other people when they are anxious. If your child can learn to tell the difference between familiar people's happy and worried faces, he can learn that familiar people's happy faces are a sign that they are safe, and their anxiety will decrease.

On page 40 of the Worry Activity Booklet there is a picture of a blank face. You will also need pencils and some books and magazines with pictures of worried faces. It can also be helpful to have photographs of your child and people he loves and likes showing worried facial expressions.

Begin the activity by showing your child pictures and photographs of worried faces. Ask your child to point out what makes these faces worried. Point out to your child that a worried face has:

- ✓ high eyebrows
- ✓ wrinkles on the forehead
- ✓ wide eyes
- ✓ an open mouth.

When your child seems to really understand what makes a worried face, ask him to make one for you. You can also ask him to make a worried face in the mirror or make a video or photograph of his worried face. Next, ask him to draw a worried face in his activity booklet. Give your child praise and encouragement at each step in this activity.

Learning to Identify Worry Through the Worried Body Signs Activity

The thermometer activity aims to help children to better recognize their anxiety by being more aware of the triggers of their anxiety. However, children also need to be able to recognize their anxiety when the trigger may not be obvious – for example, when they are in a novel situation or when their anxiety levels are slowly rising during a busy day at school. Worried body signs include feelings in the body that the child can sense. At first, children with ASD can have difficulties sensing these signs of anxiety. Some signs we can see, so many of the observable body signs also appear in the list of behavioural signs – for example, muteness. However, some cannot be seen, only felt. Once your child can sense her bodily signs of anxiety, she can identify when she is feeling 'a little worried', 'worried' and 'really worried'.

To help your child to understand the subtle experience of lower anxiety levels compared with high levels, we have included two pages in the activity booklet where Wanda describes two levels of worry: 'really worried' and 'worried'.

First, there is a page with Worried Wanda describing her 'really worried' body signs. These are:

- fast beating heart
- wide eyes
- high eyebrows
- dry mouth
- sick stomach/butterflies in the stomach
- shaky legs and hands
- tense muscles
- fast breathing
- sweating hands
- feeling the need to go to the toilet
- crying
- feeling the need to move, jiggle or fiddle (e.g. pace the room, jiggle legs up and down, or fiddle with a toy)
- feeling frozen, hard to move or speak.

Then, on the next page, Worried Wanda describes her body signs of feeling worry. These include:

- tense muscles
- dry mouth
- feeling the need to jiggle her legs
- feeling the need to fiddle with her toys.

Description of the Activity

To begin the Worried Body Signs Activity, read through Worried Wanda's body signs for 'really worried', using Worried Wanda the Watermelon puppet to act this out. Then have Wanda discuss with your child her 'really worried' body signs. Next, discuss with your child Worried Wanda's 'worry' signs. Next, using the situation in which he felt a medium level of worry that you have already identified, discuss your child's own worried body signs. It may also be helpful at this stage to describe to your child the worried body signs you have experienced. Please be aware, though, that many young children with ASD are not aware of their worried body signs. If this is the case, you can talk more generally about worried signs that most people feel.

On the next page, there is an outline of a body and boxes containing each of the worried body signs. For this activity ask your child to choose a situation that caused him to feel 'worried'. Next, help your child to draw arrows from the worried body sign boxes to the area in the body where each is felt. It is common for children to identify either the body signs for 'really worried' for this activity, or not to have noticed their body signs. Based on your own observations of your child's medium level of worry, help him to identify these body signs. Give examples where possible.

Learning to Challenge Unrealistic Worry Through the 'False Alarm vs Real Alarm' Activity[AQ]

Earlier, in Stage 1, we discussed that anxiety is a survival mechanism that has evolved in humans to help us survive life-threatening danger. If a person really is in a dangerous situation – that is, a 'real alarm' situation – then the anxiety response serves them well. However, the anxiety response also occurs when a person believes there is danger when in fact there is minimal or no risk – a 'false alarm' situation. If your child has problematic levels of anxiety, then she is, most likely, frequently experiencing anxiety in response to false alarms. Even at this early age, understanding the difference between real alarms and false alarms can help children to change their thinking and reduce their anxiety. There is an activity in the Child Worry Activity Book to explain 'Real Alarms' and 'False Alarms to your child on pages 44 and 45.

On the next page of the Worry Activity Booklet is the 'Real Alarm vs False Alarm' Story and Activity. Reintroduce your child to Worried Wanda, ensuring she is happy to see your child. Then read first the 'Real Alarm' story to your child. Next, complete the 'Real Alarm' Activity with your child by writing or drawing 'Real Alarm' situations for your child. On the next page repeat the process for 'False Alarms'.

Activity: Preparing for the 'Real Alarm' and 'False Alarm' Activities

Before completing the 'Real Alarm' and 'False Alarm' Activities, it is helpful to think of some real alarms and false alarms for your child. These might include the following.

Real alarms:

- the kitchen being on fire
- standing in the middle of the road as a car approaches
- swimming alone.

False alarms:

- having a new teacher
- meeting new people
- being separated from Mum or Dad to go to school
- sleeping in bed alone.

Write down more ideas for real alarms and false alarms for your child below:

Ideas for real alarms:

Ideas for false alarms:

_____

_____

_____

Thought Tools from the Emotional Toolbox

In Stage 7 you will also introduce your child to another set of tools from the Emotional Toolbox, Thought Tools. As we discussed in Stage 1, we know that the way we think impacts the way we feel, which in turn affects our behaviour. When faced with challenges, children with anxiety problems often overestimate the likelihood that something bad will happen to them and underestimate their ability to cope. These kinds of thoughts contribute to their feelings of anxiety and a tendency to avoid certain situations and tasks. Fortunately, children and adults alike can learn to change some of their thoughts and in turn change their emotions and behaviours. In fact, there are many different thought techniques that have demonstrated effectiveness in managing feelings of anxiety, sadness and anger. In Stage 7 you will introduce your child to one of these techniques that is especially helpful for managing anxiety: positive self-talk. Positive self-talk involves thinking about ourselves and the situation we are in, in a realistic and helpful manner. Positive self-talk can:

- reduce anxiety
- reduce avoidance behaviours
- increase coping behaviours
- improve self-esteem.

Preparing for the Thought Tools Activity

The Thought Tools Activity involves reading a story about Worried Wanda using Strong Thoughts to help her when she feels worried. Worried Wanda first explains that thoughts are words you say to yourself in your head.

She then goes on to explain that when she is worried, she needs to use her Thought Tools to help her feel brave and to have a go. She describes that it is best to use Thought Tools at the lower levels of worry. The activity next involves helping your child to make his own Strong Thoughts cards to use as Thought Tools.

To begin the activity, read through the story, using the Worried Wanda puppet to act it out. Then help your child to make their own Strong Thoughts cards. It can be helpful to make different cards for different situations or fears. Here are the instructions for making the cards:

Making Strong Thoughts Cards

1. Have ready some light-coloured blank cards that are about the size of a large business card (available from newsagencies) and a black felt-tip pen or calligraphy pen. Also have available glitter and stickers to decorate these cards if your child enjoys this sort of activity.
2. With your child, brainstorm some sayings that you tend to say to him, or he may say to himself, when he needs to be reminded of how strong he is, or when he just needs encouragement. For example, 'I am strong', 'I can do this!', 'I have got this!'
3. Choose a couple of statements that seem to be those he likes the most. Make these positive statements, like those in the example – that is, statements that say something is already true. Avoid statements that describe the behaviour you do not want – for example, 'I am not afraid' or 'I am not going to be scared'. Positive statements remind our minds of what we are capable of and make the behaviour we describe more likely.
4. Write your chosen statements on the blank cards.

Assisting Your Child to Practise Thought Tools (Strong Thoughts Cards)

Once you have created the Strong Thoughts cards, it is important to encourage your child to use these cards throughout the day, especially when she is feeling good and when she is feeling 'a little worried'. As your child becomes more and more familiar with Thought Tools, you can also help her to remember her Strong Thoughts in the moment when she is faced with higher levels of worry or anxiety. However, as you know yourself, when we are in the middle of a lot of anxiety, using Strong Thoughts to cope can be very challenging. At these times, your child may benefit from other Tools in the Toolbox in addition to your own encouragement of her.

Using Thought Tools Yourself and Modelling Thought Tools

The more you practise using Thought Tools yourself, the more you will be able to:

- ✓ stay calm during difficult situations
- ✓ easily and confidently teach your child how to use the tools
- ✓ model effective emotion regulation to your child.

Activity: Creating Your Own Plan to Use Thought Tools

Refer to the activity above where you noted your own triggers for feeling 'a little worried', 'worried' and 'really worried'. Think about each situation, thought or experience that makes you feel worried. Next, think about what thought or which words would help you to feel better. Make a list of your own Strong Thoughts below.

Trigger to worry	Strong Thought
I cannot cope with one more meltdown today. I will hit my child and never forgive myself.	I am OK. I have got this. I have coped in these situations before.

Show your child when you are using your own Thought Tools by speaking your Strong Thoughts out loud. Please note: It is very important not to share your worried thoughts, as these are likely to increase your child's anxiety. When sharing your worry, only describe how it is affecting your body and your breathing, then share how you are using Strong Thoughts to cope. Using the above example, the script may look like this:

> I just noticed that I am beginning to feel a little worried. My shoulders feel tight and my heart is beating a bit faster. I am going to use Thought Tools to calm myself down.

> I am OK. I have got this. I have coped in these situations before.

> Aaah. I feel much braver. Now I can face this situation.

As with previous tools, remember to adjust this script to suit your style and your child's level of understanding.

Weekly Plan Stage 7

The first goal for this week's Weekly Plan is to start teaching your child about the emotion worry. You will explore the various levels of worried that she experiences, how worried she feels in her body, how to recognize worried faces and the difference between helpful and unhelpful worry. The second goal is to start teaching your child how to use Thought Tools. The third goal for this Weekly Plan is to practise the next step from your child's Exposure Ladder.

Your Weekly Plan involves preparing for, scheduling and then completing the following activities with your child:

1. Meeting Worried Wanda
2. Exploring different levels of worried with the Worried Thermometer
3. We Are All Different
4. Mr Face
5. Worried Body Signs
6. Real Alarms vs False Alarms
7. Thought Tools
8. Assisting Your Child to Practise Thought Tools
9. Modelling Thought Tools
10. Practising the Exposure Ladder step.

Actions

Using the Weekly Plan, pencil in times to complete the Worry Activity Booklet with your child this week (Activities 1–7). Remember, it is important to choose a time when your child is well rested, has eaten and is not upset about anything. Then, over the next week, at these scheduled times, complete each of the six tasks in the activity booklet with your child.

Once you have completed Activity 6, schedule several times during the week to practise using Thought Tools by making more Strong Thoughts cards.

At different times during the week try to notice when you or your child are feeling worried. If you are worried, tell your child what level of worry you are experiencing, what body signs you are experiencing, and whether the situation you are worried about is a real alarm or false alarm. If your child appears worried, ask him what level of worry he is experiencing, what body signs he is experiencing, and whether the situation he is in is a real alarm or false alarm. If your child has difficulties answering these questions, help him by making suggestions (e.g. 'I think you might be feeling worried because your eyes look wide, you have stopped talking, and you want me to hug you'). It is OK if your child does not agree with you; the goal is to have your child try to tune in to his emotions and body.

Over the week, when you notice your anxiety levels rising, model to your child how you calm down using Thought Tools.

Using your Weekly Plan, pencil in times that may be good times to complete a step on your child's Exposure Ladder. If your child did not master last week's step on his Exposure Ladder, then practise this step again. If your child did master last week's step on his Exposure Ladder, then move on to the next step. Over the next week, at these scheduled times, practise this step with your child. Finally, complete the Exposure Ladder Practice Monitoring Form.

Frequently Asked Questions

What if my child insists that she is not worried about anything or she refuses to complete the Worry Thermometer Activity?
Occasionally during the worry activities, children will deny experiencing anxiety in situations that you bring up or may deny ever experiencing any anxiety whatsoever. There can be several reasons why children may do this. Often when we talk about the things that cause us anxiety, we start to feel anxious. Therefore, your child may be trying to avoid feeling anxious by trying to avoid thinking or talking about her fears. Your child may also have a poor awareness of and insight into her anxiety triggers, and thus be unable to report any situations in which she has felt anxious (instead, she may only recognize situations in which she felt 'bad' or which she 'did not like'). Finally, your child may identify with narratives in stories or movies that feeling anxiety is negative (i.e. only 'cry babies' or 'scaredy cats' feel anxious). Regardless, it is best to normalize that everyone experiences anxiety, but it can be very difficult to talk about. Refocus your conversations on your own and other people's fears and worried body signs. At the same time, keep observing closely for situations in which your child may feel anxiety. Then, once your child has become comfortable talking about other people's anxiety, have a conversation about the anxiety you noticed your child experience in the situations you observed.

What if my child cannot identify any of his own worried body signs?
Many children with ASD find it difficult to identify their worried body signs. If
this is the case for your child, again refocus your conversation on the body
signs that most people experience. When you observe that your child is experiencing anxiety in a situation, it can also be helpful to ask your child to tune
in to his body and notice what is happening. You can even ask your child if he
is experiencing each of the worried body signs or any feelings in each of the
body parts where the worried body signs are experienced.

What if my child will not talk about 'real alarms'?
Children are usually quite comfortable talking about situations that are
physically dangerous. All families teach their children about situations that
are dangerous, and most children have helpful fears about these situations.
However, if your child becomes very anxious or preoccupied with 'real alarm'
situations, it can be helpful to state that you have taken all the precautions to
ensure those situations do not occur, so we do not need to worry about them.

Exposure Ladder Practice Monitoring Form

Day	Exposure Ladder step practised	Successfully practised (i.e. your child remained in the situation until their anxiety decreased) Y/N	Comments
1			
2			
3			
4			
5			
6			
7			

Thought Tools Practice Monitoring Form

Day	Thought Tools practised	Comments
1		
2		
3		
4		
5		
6		
7		

STAGE 8

Relaxation

Overview of Stage 8

The aim of Stage 8 is to introduce activities that you can use to teach your child about the emotional state of *relaxation*. You will also learn about another set of tools from the child Emotional Toolbox, Relaxation Tools, and activities you can use to teach your child how to use Relaxation Tools.

During Stage 8 you will learn:

✓ Relaxation Awareness Tools:
  – Activities you can use to teach your child about relaxation and the different intensities at which relaxation can be felt.
  – Activities you can use to teach your child about the body signs indicating relaxation.
  – Activities you can use to teach your child to identify relaxation in others.
  – Activities you can use to teach your child about other people's perspectives, thoughts and feelings.
✓ Relaxation Tools:
  – Activities you can use to teach your child to use relaxed breathing.
  – Activities you can use to teach your child to use progressive muscle relaxation.
  – Activities you can use to teach your child to use visualization to be able to relax.
✓ The Weekly Plan.

You will need:

- ✓ Your monitoring sheets from Stage 7.
- ✓ Relaxed Ryan the Raspberry cut-out-and-colour-in puppet or a store-bought raspberry puppet.
- ✓ Scissors and glue.
- ✓ Colouring pencils and pens.
- ✓ Books, magazines or photographs of people showing relaxed facial expressions.
- ✓ The Relaxation Activity Booklet.
- ✓ This book.

Reflect on Weekly Plan Stage 7

In last week's Weekly Plan we asked you to:

1. complete the Worry Activity Booklet with your child
2. practise using Thought Tools
3. practise a step on your child's Exposure Ladder.

Completing the Worry Activity Booklet

What successes did you encounter when completing the Worry Activity Booklet with your child? Which activities did you and your child enjoy? Which new concepts was your child able to understand?

What challenges did you encounter when completing the Worry Activity Booklet? Were there any activities your child did not enjoy, or concepts that your child had difficulty understanding? How can you revisit the concepts your child had difficulty understanding?

Thought Tools
What successes did you encounter when practising the Thought Tools with your child?

What challenges did you encounter when practising the Thought Tools with your child?

Exposure Ladder
Which Exposure Ladder step did you practise with your child?

Did your child master this step? Is your child ready to move on to the next step on her Exposure Ladder? Remember, your child has mastered a step and is ready to move on to the next step on her Exposure Ladder once her anxiety has reduced significantly (i.e. reduced by at least 50%).

What successes did you encounter when preparing your child for the step, practising the step with your child and rewarding your child for practising the step?

What challenges did you face before, during and after practising the exposure hierarchy step with your child?

Based on your learning from the last week, is there anything you will approach differently this week when you complete the Relaxation Activity Booklet and Exposure Ladder step, and practise Relaxation Tools?

Top Tip

If you are feeling overwhelmed by how much your child has to learn and the slow pace of learning, take heart: you are in exactly the right place! There is a lot to learn, not just for your child but for both of you. We find a food analogy useful. Imagine how you would feel if you saw all the food that you needed to eat in a year piled on a table in front of you. The sight would be overwhelming and you would not want to start eating it all. However, if you eat a little of the food 3–5 times a day, the goal of eating all of it will be accomplished within a year. Use the strategies to teach your child a little and often, and you will meet your goal.

Introducing Relaxed Ryan the Raspberry

Relaxed Ryan the Raspberry is the character that will be used to introduce relaxation to your child. In Appendix B, you will find a cut-out-and-colour-in Relaxed Ryan the Raspberry finger puppet. On the first page of the Relaxation Activity Booklet, you will find a picture of Relaxed Ryan and a short paragraph in which Relaxed Ryan introduces himself. This paragraph reads:

Hi, I'm Relaxed Ryan the Raspberry and I feel relaxed. When I feel relaxed, my mouth smiles a small smile, my face is loose and sometimes I shut my eyes. When I feel relaxed, my body feels light and I feel as if I might float away. Sometimes I become so relaxed that I fall asleep! I feel relaxed after someone has read a nice story to me. I feel relaxed after I've had a bubble bath. I love feeling relaxed.

As with the previous emotions, read through the introduction with your child, using the finger puppet to act it out. Give Relaxed Ryan his own unique voice and compare what makes him relaxed with what makes your child relaxed.

Ideas for discussing Relaxed Ryan:

- ✓ Use a relaxed, slow and steady voice for Relaxed Ryan.
- ✓ Make Relaxed Ryan's movements soft and slow.
- ✓ Ensure your child understands the difference between happy activities (enjoyable activities that raise his heart rate and make him feel excited) and relaxing activities (enjoyable activities that decrease his heart rate and make him feel relaxed).
- ✓ Ensure that, as Relaxed Ryan, you ask your child questions about what makes him relaxed and you listen to his answers.
- ✓ Remember to follow your child's lead.

Exploring Relaxation Using a Feelings Thermometer

A Feelings Thermometer will again be used to facilitate a discussion on the activities, sights, memories and sounds that make your child 'a little relaxed', 'relaxed' and 'really relaxed'.

Using Relaxed Ryan's voice, act out Relaxed Ryan telling your child that he would like to know more about your child's feelings of relaxation, including what makes your child feel 'a little relaxed', 'relaxed' and 'really relaxed'. Next, find pictures of people and animals looking relaxed, from magazines, photographs and the internet. Cut out and glue each relaxed picture on the thermometer, at the level that your child thinks it should go. Next, encourage your child to draw or write more of her relaxation triggers on the corresponding 'a little relaxed', 'relaxed' and 'really relaxed' pages. Throughout the activity also discuss with your child what makes you feel 'a little relaxed', 'relaxed' and 'really relaxed'.

Keep in mind that many young children do not have much experience with the feeling of relaxation and commonly misinterpret happiness and relaxation as being the same feeling. It is important to keep pointing out to your child that happy activities are activities that give your child positive feelings, slightly increase her heart rate and give her energy, whereas relaxing activities are activities that give your child positive feelings, decrease her heart rate and slow her body down.

Activity: Preparing for the Relaxation Thermometer Activity

For this activity, it will be important for you to have a few suggestions about what relaxes your child so that you are ready to contribute, if necessary. Below, write down ideas about what makes your child 'a little relaxed', 'relaxed' and 'really relaxed'.

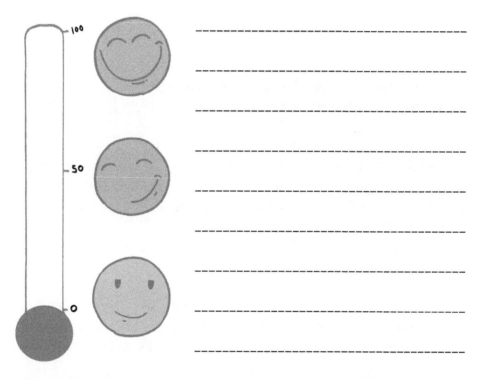

Next, write down your own ideas for what makes *you* relaxed across each of the three levels of relaxation, and consider what you feel comfortable sharing from your list with your child.

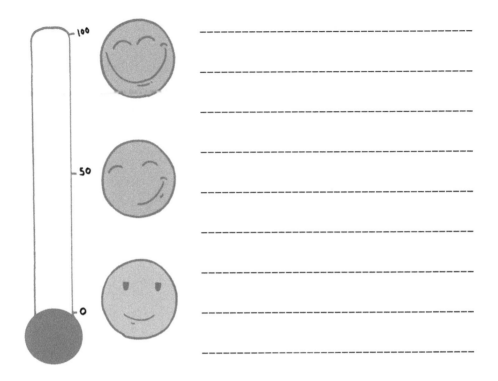

Exploring Other People's Perspectives Through the 'We Are All Different' Activity

As in the other activity booklets, the next activity in your child's activity booklet is called 'We Are All Different'. The 'We Are All Different' Activity is designed to help your child to learn that sometimes other people have the same thoughts and feelings as he does, but sometimes others have thoughts and feelings that are different to his own.

On page 56 of the Relaxation Activity Booklet there is space for you or your child to write:

- one thing that makes you and your child relaxed
- one thing that makes your child relaxed but does not make you relaxed
- one thing that makes you relaxed but does not make your child relaxed.

Read through each of these questions with your child, discuss potential answers, then write these answers in the booklet.

Activity: Preparing for the 'We Are All Different' Activity

It is helpful to have some suggestions ready for potential answers in the 'We Are All Different' Activity.

What activities or triggers lead you and your child to feel the feeling of relaxation?

What activities or triggers lead your child to feel the feeling of relaxation, but not you?

What activities or triggers lead you to feel the feeling of relaxation, but not your child?

Learning to Identify Relaxed Facial Expressions Through the 'Mr Face' Activity

The next activity in your child's workbook is 'Mr Face'. As with the other 'Mr Face' activities, you will need some pencils and some photographs and pictures of relaxed faces, perhaps from the internet, books or magazines.

Begin the activity by showing your child pictures and photographs of relaxed faces. Ask your child to point out what makes these faces relaxed. Point out to your child that a relaxed face has:

✓ low eyebrows
✓ no tension in the muscles of the face
✓ no wrinkles between the eyes on the forehead
✓ partly closed or 'soft' eyes
✓ a small smile.

Once your child understands what a relaxed face looks like, ask her to make a relaxed face for you, or make a relaxed face in the mirror, or make a video or photograph of a relaxed face. Then ask your child to draw a relaxed face in her Relaxation Activity Booklet.

Learning to Identify Relaxation Through the Relaxed Body Signs Activity

Children need to be able to recognize their body's signs of relaxation. Relaxed body signs are physiological signs that your body is calming down and a threat has passed. Once your child can notice and attend to these body signs, the state of relaxation is more likely.

On page 58 of the Relaxation Activity Booklet, Relaxed Ryan describes his relaxed body signs. These include:

- slow, regular heartbeat
- relaxed eyes and jaw
- calm tummy
- soft, heavy muscles in the arms and legs
- soft muscles generally
- slow breathing
- dry hands.

Before starting the activity, become familiar with the relaxed body signs. Think of a time when your child was experiencing a moderate to high level of relaxation. How did he look? What did you notice about his body at that time? Did he comment on how his body was feeling?

To begin the Relaxed Body Signs Activity, read through Relaxed Ryan's body signs using the raspberry puppet to act it out. Then have Relaxed Ryan discuss with your child his relaxed body signs. Remember to discuss with your child the situation in which he felt relaxed that you have already identified. However, keep in mind that many young children with ASD are not aware of any of their relaxed body signs. If your child does not remember this situation, or is struggling to identify his own signs of relaxation, talk more generally about the relaxed body signs most people feel. It will also be helpful at this stage to point out to your child the relaxed body signs that you have experienced yourself.

Then, on the next page, help your child to draw arrows from the relaxed body sign boxes to the area in the body where each is felt.

Top Tip

Later in the week, once you have taught your child the three relaxation strategies, revisit the Relaxed Body Signs Activity. Your child may be able to add to her list of relaxed body signs.

Relaxation Tools from the Emotional Toolbox

As with previous stages of *Fun with Feelings*, you will introduce a new set of Emotional Tools from the Emotional Toolbox to your child. These are Relaxation Tools. Relaxation Tools are strategies that reduce your child's feelings of anxiety or anger and increase their feelings of relaxation. Relaxation Tools work by switching on the body's parasympathetic nervous system. This is a physiological system that is built into everyone's body. It is a very handy system to have because it switches off the body's 'fight, flight or freeze' response (anxiety). There are many different relaxation tools that have been discovered in research trials to be effective for switching on the parasympathetic nervous system, thus allowing the person to manage their feelings of anxiety and anger. In this stage of the *Fun with Feelings* programme, you will introduce your child to three of these techniques:

- ✓ relaxed breathing
- ✓ progressive muscle relaxation
- ✓ guided visualization.

Introducing Relaxed Breathing

The first Relaxation Tool is relaxed breathing. Relaxed breathing induces feelings of relaxation and calms the mind by switching on the body's relaxation system, also known as the parasympathetic nervous system, as described above. Essentially, relaxed breathing changes the levels of oxygen and carbon dioxide in the blood, which in turn switches on the body's system responsible for calming down and stopping the 'fight, flight or freeze' response. Relaxed breathing is helpful when your child is starting to become anxious or angry or in situations in which they need to be calm, such as before bed.

Three skills are involved in relaxed breathing:

1. breathing in through the nose and out through the mouth
2. making the out-breath longer than the in-breath
3. moving the abdominal muscles during breathing (instead of the chest muscles).

Each of the breathing activities in the Relaxation Activity Booklet aims to teach your child these skills.

Smell the Flower and Blow Out the Candle

The first activity, 'Smell the Flower and Blow Out the Candle', aims to help your child to learn to breathe in through their nose and out through their mouth.

On page 61 of the Relaxation Activity Booklet, there are instructions which read:

1. Pretend you are holding a flower in your left hand.
2. Pretend you are holding a candle in your right hand.
3. Breathe in through your nose, pretending to smell the flower.
4. Breathe out through your mouth, pretending to blow out the candle.

Read the instructions to your child first, then complete each action with your child. Some children also enjoy completing this activity with a real flower and an (unlit) candle. Keep practising until you are sure your child has mastered this skill.

Deflate the Beach Ball

The second activity, 'Deflate the Beach Ball', aims to help your child learn to breathe out for longer than they breathe in. Breathing out for longer than we breathe in sends a strong signal to the body that it is OK to relax, the danger is over.

On page 62 of the Relaxation Activity Booklet there are instructions which read:

1. Take a normal breath in through your nose.
2. Now imagine there is a giant inflatable beach ball in your tummy. Let all the air out of your ball slowly and steadily as you breathe out.

Read all the instructions to your child, then complete each action with your child. Many young children will attempt to breathe the air out of their lungs quickly by blowing as hard as they can. If this occurs, remind your child that we want to let the air out of the beach ball slowly, not quickly. It can also be helpful to get a beach ball and show your child how the air flows out of a beach ball slowly when the valve is open. Another helpful idea for children who enjoy competition is to see who can breathe out for the longest time.

Take Your Favourite Toy for a Ride

The third activity, 'Take Your Favourite Toy for a Ride', aims to teach your child to use their abdominal muscles to breathe instead of their chest muscles.

On page 63 of the Relaxation Activity Booklet, the instructions for the activity read:

1. Lie on your back on the floor.
2. Place your toy on top of your belly button.
3. Take a normal breath in while moving your tummy muscles out.
4. Let all the air out of your lungs slowly while moving your tummy muscles in.
5. Keep practising and watch to see whether your toy moves up and down.

Read all the instructions to your child, then complete each action with them.

Introducing Progressive Muscle Relaxation

The second Relaxation Tool is progressive muscle relaxation. Progressive muscle relaxation is called 'Tense and Relaxed Muscles' in the Relaxation Activity Booklet to be more understandable for young children. As we discussed in Stage 1, muscle tension is a sign of anxiety. Children with high levels of anxiety are often tense in their bodies but they don't notice it.

Tension in the muscles can actually increase feelings of anxiety and in time lead to feelings of fatigue and even exhaustion. Luckily, the opposite is also true: relaxing the muscles can induce feelings of relaxation and calm the mind. Progressive muscle relaxation will increase your child's awareness of how her muscles feel when she is tense and the difference between that and when she is relaxed. Progressive muscles relaxation will also teach your child how to relax her muscles when they are tense.

Progressive muscle relaxation can be used daily to decrease your child's overall anxiety or stress level. It is also helpful when your child is starting to become anxious or angry or in situations in which she needs to be calm, such as before bed. Progressive muscle relaxation can also be used in combination with relaxed breathing.

On page 64 of the Relaxation Activity Booklet there is a child-friendly progressive muscle relaxation script entitled 'Recipe for Making Juice'. Read this script to your child and complete the actions with her.

Introducing Guided Visualization

The third Relaxation Tool is visualization. Visualization is called 'Imagination' in the Relaxation Activity Booklet to be more understandable for young children. Visualization helps your child to relax by focusing and calming their thoughts.

Visualization can be used daily to decrease your child's overall anxiety or stress level. Visualization is also helpful in situations in which your child needs to be calm. We find it is particularly useful for children who experience difficulties falling asleep because of their worry thoughts.

On page 65 of the Relaxation Activity Booklet is a guided relaxation script that describes a beach scene. However, your child can imagine any calm place he likes – for example, a forest, a lake or a quiet room. The important thing is to focus on the sensory details of the place – the gentle sounds, the pleasant smells, the sights and what he can touch.

Practising Relaxation Tools

Your Weekly Plan this week includes practising these techniques with your child a number of times – daily if possible. Learning to relax is just like learning any skill: we need to practise it in order to be able to do it easily.

During the time that your child is still learning Relaxation Tools, encourage her to practise these techniques only when she is already quite happy and/or relaxed. It will be too overwhelming for your child to learn a new skill while she is feeling anxious or angry. It is also helpful, when your child first starts learning to use Relaxation Tools, to practise using the tools only in places that are already very relaxing for your child such as her own bed at home, your bed, a cubby house or a special 'relaxation' space in your home. As your child becomes more familiar with the Relaxation Tools, move on to practising using the tools in other places that are not as relaxing such as in the car or kitchen. And remember, children with ASD thrive when their routines are predictable, so add relaxation practice to their daily visual schedule and give them advance warning of practice times.

Using Relaxation Tools Yourself

As always, it is important that you practise using Relaxation Tools yourself so that you can:

- ✓ stay calm during difficult situations
- ✓ more easily and confidently teach your child how to use the tools
- ✓ model effective emotion regulation to your child.

It would be very helpful for you to learn how to use progressive muscle relaxation yourself, either before or while teaching this skill to your child. To assist you to do this, use one of the many audio recordings created for this purpose on the internet. One that two of the authors of *Fun with Feelings* have created for adults is available on the Attwood & Garnett website (www.attwoodandgarnettevents.com) under Resources on the Tab Menu, and under 'Tools' on the dropdown menu.

Modelling Using Relaxation Tools to Your Child

It is also important to model effective emotion regulation to your child by demonstrating effective use of the Relaxation Tools. When you are feeling anxious, stressed or tense, model using Relaxation Tools with the following script:

> I just noticed that I am beginning to feel a little worried. My shoulders feel tight. I am going to use a breathing tool to calm myself down.

Next, show your child you are using one of the breathing tools as described above and say:

> Aaah. I feel much calmer now. When I am calm, I am smarter and I can cope.

As with previous tools, remember to adjust this script to suit your style and your child's level of understanding.

Encouraging Your Child to Use Relaxation Tools When They Experience Anxiety or Anger

As with all the strategies we are using, once you have taught your child how to use the Relaxation Tools, and she has practised them when not feeling anxious, it is important to encourage your child to use the strategies when she is feeling anxious. Equally, it is important that you help your child to use the Relaxation Tools and you use the Relaxation Tools alongside your child. The Relaxation Tools work best when your child is feeling a little worried, a little angry, worried or angry.

Weekly Plan Stage 8

The first goal for this week's Weekly Plan is to start teaching your child about the emotional state of relaxation, including the various levels of relaxation that he experiences, how relaxation feels in the body, how to recognize relaxed faces, and that people differ in what makes them relaxed. The second goal for this Weekly Plan is to start teaching your child how to use Relaxation Tools. The third goal for this Weekly Plan is to practise a step from your child's Exposure Ladder.

Your Weekly Plan involves preparing for, scheduling and then completing the following activities with your child:

1. Meeting Relaxed Ryan

2. Exploring different levels of relaxation with the Relaxation Thermo-meter
3. We Are All Different
4. Mr Face
5. Relaxed Body Signs
6. Relaxed Breathing
7. Progressive Muscle Relaxation
8. Guided Visualization
9. Daily practice of Awareness Tools
10. Daily practice of Relaxation Tools
11. Modelling use of Relaxation Tools
12. Practising the Exposure Ladder step.

Action

Using the Weekly Plan, pencil in times to complete the Relaxation Activity Booklet with your child this week. Then, over the next week, at these scheduled times, complete each of the eight activities in the activity booklet with your child.

Once you have completed the activity booklet, schedule 2–10 minutes each day to practise a Relaxation Tool with your child when he is already calm and/or happy. Use the self-monitoring sheet at the end of the Relaxation Activity Booklet for your child to record how he felt before using the Relaxation Tool and afterwards. He can record this using faces.

Throughout the week try to notice when you or your child are feeling relaxed. If you are relaxed, tell your child what level of relaxation you are experiencing and what body signs you are experiencing. If your child appears relaxed, ask him what level of relaxation he is experiencing and what relaxation body signs he is experiencing.

On a daily basis, when you notice a change in your stress levels and you are feeling more tense, model to your child how you calm down, using one of the three relaxation strategies.

Using the Weekly Plan, select a step from your child's Exposure Ladder and pencil in times that may be good times to practise this step. If your child did not master this week's step on their Exposure Ladder, then practise this step again. If your child did master this week's step on their Exposure Ladder, then move on to the next step. Then, over the next week, at these scheduled times, practise this step with your child. Finally, complete the Exposure Ladder Practice Monitoring Form.

Frequently Asked Questions

What if my child is resistant to learning the relaxation strategies and is very negative?

This is quite a common problem. Children with ASD are unlikely to embrace anything new. They can find it threatening and may well prefer avoidance to learning how to deal with the uncomfortable feelings of anxiety. They also prefer to discover ideas for themselves, rather than receive advice or guidance from others. It is part of their self-directed learning style. If this happens, we recommend initially decoupling learning to relax from anxiety. Instead, talk about feeling even more calm or even more relaxed. Model this to your child rather than using relaxation for tension or anxiety. Say to your child, 'Isn't it lovely to feel relaxed? I love feeling calm. Now I feel a little relaxed, I am going to use calming breathing to help me feel even more relaxed.' Ask her, 'What do you do to feel relaxed?' Tell her how smart she is for knowing what relaxes her. Tell her how smart her body is, for knowing how to relax on her own when given the right activities.

Another reason for resistance is the child explaining that when she tries to relax and 'clear her mind of worries', the worries seem to intrude even more and spiral out of control. This can occur with children whose primary means of coping with anxiety is engaging in rituals, routines and a special interest. To encourage relaxation as an effective tool, you will need to emphasize guided visualization that is vivid and feels almost real, to block worried thoughts from becoming stronger when trying to relax.

I feel tense and have rarely ever felt relaxed myself. How can I possibly help my child?

Great question! We recommend that you practise the strategies yourself first. Once you are proficient at using the strategies, it is time to teach your child. Until you have reached this step, teaching your child the strategies is unlikely to work. If it is hard to stay focused to work on your own relaxation strategies, consider doing it with a similarly anxious friend, or employ a counsellor or psychologist to help. If high levels of anxiety are an ongoing and difficult problem for you, see a clinical psychologist for yourself. This step is likely to help your child more than any other step in the programme.

Relaxation Tools Practice Monitoring Form

Day	Relaxation Tools practised	Comments
1		
2		
3		
4		
5		
6		
7		

Exposure Ladder Practice Monitoring Form

Day	Exposure Ladder step practised	Successfully practised (i.e. your child remained in the situation until their anxiety decreased) Y/N	Comments
1			
2			
3			
4			
5			
6			
7			

Anger and Physical Tools

Overview of Stage 9

The aim of Stage 9 is to introduce activities that you can use to teach your child about the emotion *anger*. You will also learn about Physical Tools and activities you can use to teach your child how to use Physical Tools.

During Stage 9 you will learn:

✓ Awareness Tools:
  – Activities you can use to teach your child about the emotion anger and the different intensities at which anger can be felt.
  – Activities you can use to teach your child about other people's perspectives, thoughts and feelings.
  – Activities you can use to teach your child to identify anger in others.
  – Activities you can use to teach your child about angry body signs.
✓ Physical Tools:
  – Activities you can use to teach your child how to use Everyday Physical Tools.
  – Activities you can use to teach your child how to use Anger-Busting Physical Tools.
✓ The Weekly Plan.

You will need:

✓ Your monitoring sheets from Stage 8.

- ✓ Angry Alan the Apple cut-out-and-colour-in puppet or a store-bought apple puppet.
- ✓ Scissors and glue.
- ✓ Colouring pencils and pens.
- ✓ Books, magazines or photographs of people showing angry facial expressions.
- ✓ The Anger Activity Booklet.
- ✓ This book.

Reflect on Weekly Plan Stage 8

In last week's Weekly Plan we asked you to:

1. complete the Relaxation Activity Booklet with your child
2. practise using Relaxation Tools
3. practise a step on your child's exposure hierarchy.

Relaxation Activity Booklet

What success did you encounter when completing the Relaxation Activity Booklet? Which activities did you and your child enjoy? Which new concepts was your child able to understand?

What challenges did you encounter when completing the Relaxation Activity Booklet? Where there any activities your child did not enjoy or concepts that your child had difficulty understanding? How can you revisit the concepts your child had difficulty understanding?

_____

_____

_____

_____

Relaxation Tools

What successes did you encounter when practising Relaxation Tools with your child?

_____

_____

_____

_____

_____

What challenges did you encounter when practising Relaxation Tools with your child?

_____

_____

_____

_____

_____

Exposure Ladder

Which Exposure Ladder step did you practise with your child?

Did your child master this step? Is your child ready to move on to the next step on their Exposure Ladder? Remember, your child has mastered their current step and is ready to move on to their next step once their anxiety has reduced significantly (i.e. reduced by at least 50%).

What successes did you encounter when preparing your child for the step, practising the step with your child and rewarding your child for practising the step?

What challenges did you face before, during and after practising the Exposure Ladder step with your child?

Based on your learning from the last week, is there anything you will approach differently this week when you complete the Anger Activity Booklet and practise Physical Tools and an Exposure Ladder step?

Introducing Angry Alan the Apple

Angry Alan the Apple is the character that will be used to introduce anger to your child. In Appendix B there is a cut-out-and-colour-in Angry Alan the Apple finger puppet. On page 68 of the Anger Activity Booklet, there is a picture of Angry Alan and a short paragraph in which Angry Alan introduces himself. This paragraph reads:

Hi, I'm Angry Alan the Apple and I feel angry. When I feel angry, my eyebrows go down, my forehead gets wrinkly and I grit my teeth. When I feel angry, my face goes red, my body feels tight, my hands want to punch, and my feet want to kick and stomp. I feel angry when someone takes my toy without asking. I feel angry when I want something and I'm not allowed to have it. I feel angry when someone tells me I'm wrong or I make a mistake. Feeling angry is not much fun. When I feel angry, I sometimes explode like a volcano and this can make other people feel scared and upset.

As with the other emotions, read through the introduction with your child, using the finger puppet to act it out. Give Angry Alan his own unique voice and compare what makes him angry with what makes you and your child angry.

Ideas for discussing Angry Alan:

- ✓ Use a halting, stern and slightly raised voice for Angry Alan.
- ✓ Encourage your child to do or say something to help Angry Alan feel less angry.
- ✓ Ensure that, as Angry Alan, you ask your child questions about what makes her angry and you listen to her answers.
- ✓ Follow your child's lead – if your child wants to be silly with Angry Alan, then be silly.

Exploring Anger Using a Feelings Thermometer

On page 69 of the Anger Activity Booklet there is a picture of Angry Alan saying:

We all feel different levels of being angry. Sometimes we are a little angry. Sometimes we are angry. Sometimes we are really angry. We can rate how angry we are feeling on the Angry Thermometer.

Use the picture of the thermometer to facilitate discussion of what makes you and your child 'a little angry', 'angry' and 'really angry'. 'A little angry' may be particularly difficult for your child to recognize in himself, so it will be important to spend a little time on this level. The activity below will prepare you for this activity. On the next pages of the Anger Activity Booklet there is space to write down the triggers for your child's anger, at each level.

Activity: Preparing for the Angry Thermometer Activity

In preparation for the Angry Thermometer Activity, write down ideas for what makes your child 'a little angry', 'angry' and 'really angry'.

Next, write down your own ideas for what makes you angry across each of the three levels of angry and consider what you feel comfortable sharing from your list with your child.

Top Tip

Children can have difficulty distinguishing between feelings of sadness and anger. It can be helpful to think of sadness as related to loss – for example, losing a toy or saying goodbye to a friend or loved one – and anger as related to injustice – for example, having a toy broken or getting in trouble for something you did not do.

Exploring Other People's Perspectives Through the 'We Are All Different' Activity

The next activity in your child's Anger Activity Booklet is called 'We Are All Different'. The 'We Are All Different' Activity is designed to help your child to learn that sometimes other people have the same thoughts and feelings as she does, but sometimes others have thoughts and feelings that are different to her own.

On page 73 of the Anger Activity Booklet there is space for you or your child to write:

- one thing that makes you and your child angry
- one thing that makes your child angry but does not make you angry
- one thing that makes you angry but does not make your child angry.

Read through each of these questions with your child, discuss potential answers, then write these answers in the booklet.

Activity: Preparing for the 'We Are All Different' Activity

It is helpful to have some suggestions ready for potential answers in the 'We Are All Different' Activity.

What makes you and your child angry?

_____

_____

What makes your child angry but does not make you angry?

_____

_____

What makes you angry but does not make your child angry?

_____

_____

Learning to Identify Facial Expression Through the 'Mr Face' Activity

The next activity in your child's workbook is Mr Face.

On page 74 of the Anger Activity Booklet there is a picture of a blank face. As with the other Mr Face activities, you will also need some pencils and some books and magazines with pictures of angry faces.

Begin the activity by showing your child pictures and photographs of angry faces. Ask your child to point out what makes these faces angry. Point out to your child that an angry face has smaller eyes, eyebrows down, wrinkles between the eyes, a clenched mouth and tensed muscles. Then, when your child understands what makes an angry face, ask him to make one for you. Alternatively, ask your child to make an angry face in the mirror or to make a video or a photograph of an angry face. Finally, ask your child to draw an angry face in the booklet.

Learning to Identify Angry Through the 'Angry Body Signs' Activity

Just like anxiety, anger is a very physical emotion that has a range of physical body changes or signs associated with it. Learning about angry body signs will help your child learn to identify her feelings of anger more quickly and at lower intensities and in turn help her to use appropriate emotion regulation strategies to calm herself before she reaches extreme levels of anger. You can explore situations that create different levels of anger for your child, such as being unable to do an activity, social injustice, being teased or tormented, not playing by the rules, being interrupted, taking possessions without permission, and not being listened to. These could be discussed and rated for the level of anger that they create using the thermometer.

On page 75 of the Anger Activity Booklet there is a page with Angry Alan describing his angry body signs. These are:

- eyebrows down
- forehead gets wrinkly
- gritted teeth
- hot face
- body feels tight
- muscles feel tense
- feel angry energy
- voice gets louder
- heart beats fast
- hands want to punch
- legs want to kick
- stomp feet.

Then, on the next page, there is an outline of a body and boxes containing each of the angry body signs. Before you start the activity, think of a recent time when your child felt anger and you observed some of his angry body signs.

To begin the Angry Body Signs Activity, read through Angry Alan's body signs using the apple puppet to act it out. Then have Angry Alan discuss with your child his angry body signs. Remember to also discuss with your child the situation in which he felt angry that you have already identified. It may also be helpful at this stage to point out to your child angry body signs that you have experienced. Please be aware, though, that many young children with ASD are not aware of their angry body signs. If this is the case, you can talk more generally about angry body signs that most people feel.

On the next page, help your child to draw arrows from the angry body sign boxes to the area in the body where each is felt.

Physical Tools from the Emotional Toolbox

The next set of tools in the Emotional Toolbox is Physical Tools. Physical Tools are physical activities that release negative emotional energy, induce feelings of happiness and relaxation, and calm and focus the mind. A Physical Tool is any activity that gets your child moving and increases her heart rate. Physical Tools can be anything from stomping on boxes to tearing up paper, to jumping on a trampoline, to playing a team sport. In Stage 9 you will introduce your child to two types of Physical Tools:

- ✓ Everyday Physical Tools
- ✓ Anger-Busting Physical Tools.

Introducing Everyday Physical Tools

Regular physical activity can have many benefits for your child's emotional well-being. When we engage in physical activity, our brain releases endorphins, a group of hormones that act like opiates in the brain, inducing feelings of happiness and well-being. Regular physical activity has been shown to be more effective than medication for alleviating mild anxiety and depression. Moreover, regular physical activity increases coordination, confidence and self-esteem. Thus, your child's overall level of anxiety may reduce and his overall happiness increase by engaging in regular physical activity.

On page 77 of the Anger Activity Booklet, there is a story in which Angry Alan explains that completing a Physical Tool every day helps him to feel happy, strong and confident. Then, on the next pages, there are suggestions for Everyday Physical Tools your child can try.

To begin the activity, read through the story using the Angry Alan puppet to act it out. Then, on the next page, help your child to circle Everyday

Physical Tools he already does and enjoys or Everyday Physical Tools your child thinks he may enjoy and would like to try.

Activity: Physical Tools My Child Can Use on a Regular Basis

Before completing the Physical Tools Activity, it is helpful to think of some Everyday Physical Tools that your child already completes and enjoys, as well as some Everyday Physical Tools that your child may enjoy and be open to trying. Below is a list of physical activities that may appeal to young children with ASD. Read through the list and tick off activities that you could incorporate into your child's daily and weekly routine.

- ☐ Riding a bike.
- ☐ Riding a scooter.
- ☐ Swimming.
- ☐ Jumping on a trampoline.
- ☐ Dancing.
- ☐ Running around the backyard.
- ☐ Playing on playground equipment.
- ☐ Throwing a ball.
- ☐ Playing a team sport such as soccer or baseball.
- ☐ Dance classes.
- ☐ Individual or group classes (e.g. dance class, tennis lesson, soccer skills lesson).
- ☐ Other: _____ .

Introducing Anger-Busting Physical Tools

In addition to being beneficial to overall emotional well-being, Physical Tools can also be helpful in reducing high levels of anger. Intense physical activity quickly releases negative emotional energy. After this emotional energy has been released, a person feels less angry and more relaxed, and is able to think more clearly and problem-solve more effectively. Anger-Busting Physical Tools are helpful when your child is exhibiting the 'fight' component of the 'fight, flight or freeze' response or if she is really angry about something. It can be helpful to first use Physical Tools to reduce your child's high level of anger to a lower level of anger, then to use other tools to help your child calm even further.

On page oo of the Anger Activity Booklet, there is a story in which Angry Alan explains that when he is feeling really angry, he needs to use his Anger-Busting Physical Tools to move his body and get his angry energy out. Then, on the next pages, there are suggestions for Anger-Busting Physical Tools your child can try.

To begin the activity, read through the story using the Angry Alan puppet to act it out. Have Angry Alan ask your child what makes her angry and compare what makes him angry with what makes your child angry. Also, have Angry Alan ask your child what she does when she is angry and compare what your child does when she is angry with what Angry Alan does when he is angry. Then, on the next page, help your child to circle Physical Tools she would like to try using when she is angry.

Activity: Physical Tools My Child Can Use to Reduce Her Anger

Below is a list of physical activities that will help your child safely release his negative emotional energy. Read through the list and tick off activities that may appeal to your child.

- ☐ Tearing up paper or magazines.
- ☐ Stomping on cardboard boxes.
- ☐ Squeezing a stress ball.
- ☐ Squeezing a pillow.
- ☐ Punching a pillow.
- ☐ Screaming into a pillow.
- ☐ Kicking a ball.
- ☐ Throwing a ball.
- ☐ Running around the backyard.
- ☐ Jumping on the trampoline.
- ☐ Other: _____ .

Practising Physical Tools

Everyday Physical Tools

Often children do not need to learn how to use Everyday Physical Tools; however, it is important that they use these on a daily basis to reduce negative feelings and increase feelings of happiness and confidence. It is also important that they learn to identify the effect Everyday Physical Tools can have on their emotions.

Your Weekly Plan this week includes scheduling time for your child to engage in at least one of her Everyday Physical Tools each day and helping your child to rate her feelings before and after using her Everyday Physical Tools. On the last page of the Anger Activity Booklet there is a self-monitoring sheet, providing space for your child to record her feelings before and after completing her Everyday Physical Tool, using the thermometers provided. The idea is for the child to draw the angry face to represent her feelings before using the Everyday Physical Tool, and then to draw the less angry face, or even a relaxed face, after using the tool. Some families find that removing this page from the workbook (or photocopying it) and sticking it on the fridge or a family notice board helps to remind them to complete this monitoring.

Anger-Busting Physical Tools

Just like many of the other Emotional Tools, using Anger-Busting Physical Tools requires skills that need to be practised. When you first practise Anger-Busting Physical Tools with your child, do so at a time when your child is happy. It will be too overwhelming for him to learn this new skill while feeling angry. The first couple of practices should be role plays in which you and your child role-play how your child will use Anger-Busting Physical Tools (and how you will assist him to use Anger-Busting Physical Tools) when he is angry. Once your child understands how to use Anger-Busting Physical Tools, practise using Anger-Busting Physical Tools when your child is only a little angry or angry. During this phase of practice, it is good to trial a few different Physical Tools in order to determine which tools work best for your child. As you learn the best Anger-Busting Physical Tools for your child, add these to the Anxiety Survival Plan, in Appendix A. You will notice that Physical Tools work best when your child's anger is at the higher levels; this needs to be recorded there.

Using Physical Tools Yourself

As always, it is important you practise using Physical Tools yourself so that you can:

- ✓ have lower overall levels of stress, anxiety and anger
- ✓ more easily and confidently teach your child how to use the tools
- ✓ model effective emotion regulation to your child.

Activity: Physical Tools That I Can Use to Reduce My Anger

Take a moment now to note down activities that you can use in the week as Everyday Physical Tools and Anger-Busting Physical Tools.

Everyday Physical Tools I can use:

_____

_____

_____

_____

_____

Anger-Busting Physical Tools I can use:

_____

_____

_____

_____

Modelling Using Physical Tools to Your Child

It is also important to model effective emotion regulation to your child by showing effective use of the Physical Tools. Remember, effective use of the tools does not mean a perfect performance. It is really important to show that you are trying. When you make a mistake and forget to use a tool, or the tool does not work, tell your child what happened and how you have learned from this.

When you complete an everyday physical activity, share with your child the positive feelings of happiness and confidence you experience.

When you are angry, model using Physical Tools with the following script:

> I just noticed that I am beginning to feel angry. My muscles are tensing, I feel hot, and my heart is beating faster. I am going use my Physical Tool of walking up and down the stairs to calm myself down.

Next, model walking up and down the stairs as described above, then say:

> I feel much calmer. Now I will be able to be smarter and cope better.

As with previous tools, remember to adjust this script to suit your style and your child's level of understanding.

If you forget to use a tool and lose your cool – for example, shouting at your child or saying something you regretted later – as soon as you can after the event, apologize to your child and describe what you could have done better. For example:

> I am sorry I lost my temper this morning. I forgot to use the Tools in my Toolbox. Next time, I will remember to use a Physical Tool for anger and walk up and down the stairs instead of yelling. That is OK; nobody is perfect.

Young children with ASD can be hard on themselves. Model kindness to yourself, especially when you are not your best version of yourself.

Encouraging Your Child to Use Physical Tools to Reduce High Levels of Anger

When your child is comfortable using Physical Tools and you have a list of two or three Physical Tools that work well for your child, encourage and assist your child to use Physical Tools when she is really angry. Remember, it is very important that you actively help your child to use her Physical Tools.

Weekly Plan Stage 9

The first goal for this week's Weekly Plan is to start teaching your child about the emotion anger, including the various levels of anger he experiences, how anger feels in the body, how to recognize angry faces, and that people differ in what makes them angry. The second goal for this Weekly Plan is to start teaching your child how to use Physical Tools. The third goal for this Weekly Plan is to practise another step from your child's Exposure Ladder.

Your Weekly Plan involves preparing for, scheduling and then completing the following activities with your child:

1. Meeting Angry Alan
2. Exploring different levels of anger with the Angry Thermometer
3. We Are All Different
4. Mr Face
5. Angry Body Signs
6. Everyday Physical Tools
7. Anger-Busting Physical Tools
8. Daily practice of Physical Tools
9. Modelling use of Physical Tools
10. Practising the Exposure Ladder step.

Action

Using the Weekly Plan, pencil in times that may be good times to schedule the five 2–10-minute activities with your child this week (Activities 1–7 above). Then, at these scheduled times, complete each of the activities in the Anger Activity Booklet with your child.

Once you have completed the Anger Activity Booklet, schedule 2–10 minutes each day to practise an Everyday Physical Tool with your child when she is already calm and/or happy. Use the self-monitoring sheet to track your child's emotions before and after using the Everyday Physical Tool and make any comments.

Using the Weekly Plan, also schedule 3–4 times in the week to role-play using an Anger-Busting Physical Tool. Remember, though, for the first week, these role plays need to be conducted at a time when your child is already calm or happy, so you may need to be flexible with these scheduled times.

Throughout the week, try to notice times when you or your child are feeling angry. If you are angry, tell your child what level of angry you are experiencing and what angry body signs you are experiencing. If your child appears angry, ask her to rate her level of anger and to describe her angry body signs.

Throughout the week also model using Physical Tools to reduce your anger.

Using the Weekly Plan, select a step from your child's Exposure Ladder and pencil in times that may be good times to practise this step. Then, over the next week, at these scheduled times, practise this step with your child. Finally, complete the Exposure Ladder Practice Monitoring Form.

Frequently Asked Questions

What if my child insists he does not feel angered by anything, or he refuses to complete the Angry Thermometer Activity?

Occasionally, during the anger activities children will deny experiencing anger in situations that you bring up or deny ever experiencing any anger whatsoever. There can be a number of reasons why children may do this. Often children associate being angry with getting in trouble because in the past they have been reprimanded for hitting out or saying hurtful things when angry. It is important to explain to your child that there is nothing wrong with being angry and that everyone gets angry sometimes. It is OK to be angry, but it is not OK to let your anger hurt someone else by hitting, kicking, saying hurtful things or damaging their things. A good mantra for young children is 'It is OK to be angry, but it is not OK to be mean'.

Physical Tools Practice Monitoring Form

Day	Physical Tools practised	Comments
1		
2		
3		
4		
5		
6		
7		

Exposure Ladder Practice Monitoring Form

Day	Exposure Ladder step practised	Successfully practised (i.e. your child remained in the situation until their anxiety decreased) Y/N	Comments
1			
2			
3			
4			
5			
6			
7			

Affection and Social Tools

Overview of Stage 10

The aim of Stage 10 is to introduce activities that you can use to teach your child about *love and affection*. You will also learn about Social Tools and activities you can use to teach your child how to use Social Tools.

During Stage 10 you will learn:

✓ Affection Awareness Tools:
   – Activities you can use to teach your child about affection and the different intensities affection can be felt.
   – Activities you can use to teach your child about other people's perspectives, thoughts and feelings.
   – Activities you can use to teach your child to identify affection in others.
✓ Social Tools:
   – Activities you can use to teach your child how to use Social Tools.
✓ The Weekly Plan.

You will need:

✓ Your monitoring sheets from Stage 9.
✓ Loving Lulu the Lemon cut-out-and-colour-in puppet or a store-bought lemon puppet.
✓ Scissors and glue.
✓ Colouring pencils and pens.

✓ Books, magazines or photographs of people showing faces expressing liking or love for other people or animals.
✓ The Love and Affection Activity Booklet.
✓ This book.

Reflect on Weekly Plan Stage 9

In last week's Weekly Plan we asked you to:

1. complete the Anger Activity Booklet with your child
2. practise using Everyday Physical Tools
3. practise using Anger-Busting Physical Tools
4. practise a step on your child's Exposure Ladder.

Anger Activity Booklet

What success did you encounter when completing the Anger Activity Booklet? Which activities did you and your child enjoy? Which new concepts was your child able to understand?

What challenges did you encounter when completing the Anger Activity Booklet? Were there any activities your child did not enjoy or concepts that your child had difficulty understanding? How can you revisit the concepts your child had difficulty understanding?

Physical Tools

What successes did you encounter when practising Everyday Physical Tools with your child?

What challenges did you encounter when practising Everyday Physical Tools with your child?

What successes did you encounter when role-playing using Anger-Busting Physical Tools with your child?

What challenges did you encounter when role-playing using Anger-Busting Physical Tools with your child?

Exposure Ladder

Which Exposure Ladder step did you practise with your child?

Did your child master this step? Is your child ready to move on to the next step on their Exposure Ladder? Remember, your child has mastered their current step and is ready to move on to their next step once their anxiety has reduced significantly (i.e. reduced by at least 50%).

What challenges did you face before, during and after completing the Exposure Ladder step with your child?

Based on your learnings from the last week, is there anything you will approach differently this week when you complete the Love and Affection Activity Booklet, practise an Exposure Ladder step and practise Social Tools?

Emotion Education on Affection

It may seem unusual to include affection in a book designed to assist children to manage their emotions. For children who are not on the autism spectrum, affection is often used effectively to assist them to manage their strong and difficult emotions. However, children on the autism spectrum can be confused and overwhelmed by gestures of affection, such as hugs, compliments and expressions of love. As Matthew, an 11-year-old boy with ASD, said, 'I fail to understand why the exertion of pressure on a human body could be considered comforting.' Sarah, who has ASD, was eight years old when she said, 'Don't cry, they will squeeze you.' Two of the authors of this book feel so strongly that it is helpful for children with ASD to understand and express affection that they have written two books on the topic (Attwood and Garnett, 2013a, 2013b). Learning about affection, including like and love, can open the child up to both receiving and giving affection, and thus receiving the enormous benefits associated with this skill. These benefits include feeling safe, likeable and lovable, having a sense of self-worth and a feeling of belonging. Each of these feelings decreases anxiety and anger. You can see why we could not leave affection out of a programme on feelings!

Before we start, a note on language. Because young children are often unfamiliar with the word 'affection', we have chosen to use the more familiar words 'like' and 'love' to explain affection.

Introducing Loving Lulu the Lemon

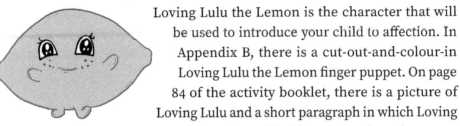

Loving Lulu the Lemon is the character that will be used to introduce your child to affection. In Appendix B, there is a cut-out-and-colour-in Loving Lulu the Lemon finger puppet. On page 84 of the activity booklet, there is a picture of Loving Lulu and a short paragraph in which Loving Lulu introduces herself. This paragraph reads:

Hi, I'm Loving Lulu the Lemon. There many people and animals that I like and some that I love. I like my friends, and I really like my best friends, Banana and Gooseberry. I like all my Feeling Friends, Henry, Sally, Ryan, Wanda and Alan. I love my teddy bear, Boo. I also love my mum and dad. It feels great to like and love my friends and family. When I feel the emotion 'liking', I feel both relaxed and happy at the same time. My face is soft and open-looking. I look friendly. When I feel the emotion 'loving', I feel the same as liking, but more strongly. I also feel safe. My teddy and my mum and dad feel happy when I show them that I love them. When they are happy, I feel happy.

As with the other emotions, read through the introduction with your child, using the finger puppet to act it out. Give Loving Lulu her own unique voice. Have Loving Lulu ask your child whom he likes and loves. Encourage your child to ask Lulu whom she likes and loves. Compare whom Lulu likes and loves to whom your child likes and loves.

Exploring Affection Using a Feelings Thermometer

As before, this activity is designed to assist you to have discussions about emotions at different levels of intensity. Use the thermometer to discuss with your child whom she 'likes a little', 'likes' and 'loves'.

Activity: Preparing for the Like/Love Thermometer Activity

In preparation for the Like/Love Thermometer Activity, write down ideas for people and animals that your child 'likes a little', 'likes' and 'loves'. Many children with ASD love and have a special affinity with animals. Do not be surprised if her sense of love for a pet exceeds the intensity of love felt for a family member! We understand that your child will identify with other activities and things that she likes or loves. The purpose of exploring affection in *Fun with Feelings* is to assist the child to recognize, understand and express affection for sentient beings with whom they may have a relationship. While these activities will help your child enormously with emotion regulation, they also provide the foundation stone for how to relate to people in a meaningful way.

Next, write down your own ideas for whom you like a little, like and love, and consider what you feel comfortable sharing from your list with your child.

```
------------------------------------------------

------------------------------------------------

------------------------------------------------

------------------------------------------------

------------------------------------------------

------------------------------------------------
```

Learning to Identify Facial Expression Through the 'Mr Face' Activity

The next activity is the 'Mr Face' Activity to assist your child to recognize the different levels of like and love in facial expressions.

On page 89 of the Love and Affection Activity Booklet there is a picture of a blank face. As with the other Mr Face activities, you will also need some pencils and some books and magazines with pictures of faces expressing liking or love for other people or animals.

Begin the activity by showing your child pictures and photographs of faces showing different levels of liking and loving. Ask your child to point out what makes a face look as though it is showing like or love. Point out to your child that faces showing affection have:

- ✓ soft eyes
- ✓ a relaxed mouth
- ✓ a smooth face.

Then, when your child understands what makes a face that conveys love or liking, ask her to make one for you. Alternatively, ask your child to make a loving face in the mirror or to make a video or a photograph of a loving face. Finally, ask your child to draw a loving face in the booklet. Make a loving face to your child and ask her to look at your face. Tell her that you look at her like this when you are feeling love for her.

Affection is one of the more difficult faces to describe in words. It can be helpful to let your child look at the eyes of people and animals that are show-ing affection, in photographs and pictures, and in real life, so that they can visually memorize what the emotion looks like. The differences in relaxed, happy and affectionate facial expressions can be difficult to describe, but easier to recognize visually. Once your child can recognize love and liking more easily in faces, she may be more comfortable with eye contact with people who use this form of non-verbal communication with her regularly.

Learning to Identify Affection Through the Like and Love Body Signs Activity

Just like any emotion, affection has its own set of body signs that tell us when we are feeling liking or love for someone or an animal. Adults tend to associate loving body signs with romantic love. When describing bodily signs of liking and loving to your young child, instead of thinking of romantic love, think about the sort of liking or love you feel for a friend, an animal, a young child or a family member who is not your partner.

On page 90 of the Love and Affection Activity Booklet, Loving Lulu the Lemon describes her body signs of liking someone, her friend Gretel the Grape. These are:

- face soft and relaxed
- jaw relaxed
- body feels relaxed
- muscles feel soft
- feel happy and calm energy
- voice is soft, more quiet
- heart rate is slowed
- hands are relaxed
- legs feel comfortable.

On the next page there is an outline of a body and boxes containing each of the like/love body signs. Before you start the activity, think of a recent time when your child felt like or love towards someone or something and you observed some of his like or love body signs.

To begin the Like and Love Body Signs Activity, read through Loving Lulu the Lemon's body signs using the lemon puppet to act it out. Then have

Loving Lulu the Lemon discuss with your child his like and love body signs. Remember to also discuss with your child the situation in which he felt like or love that you have already identified. It may also be helpful at this stage to point out to your child the like and love body signs you have experienced. Please be aware, though, that many young children with ASD are not aware of their like or love body signs. If this is the case, you can talk more generally about like and love body signs that most people feel.

On the next page, help your child to draw arrows from the like and love body sign boxes to the area in the body where each is felt.

Social Tools from the Emotions Toolbox

The final set of tools in the Emotional Toolbox is the Social Tools. We focus on three Social Tools in *Fun with Feelings*. These include:

- Spending time with a person who cares or a pet. This includes any kind of supportive, enjoyable, stress-free social interaction that occurs with another person or animal.
- Asking for help. Your child is likely to need to know how to ask for help, as well as who to go to. A script can be helpful.
- Telling someone who cares what she is feeling – for example, telling you 'I am very angry'.

To assist your child to learn to use Social Tools, you will be helping him to determine who to go to. Consider which supportive adults and children could help your child to reduce his negative feelings and increase his feelings of happiness and relaxation by:

- validating his angry, sad or anxious feelings
- expressing love or liking in a way he understands – for example, giving a compliment
- helping to generate positive self-talk
- helping to solve a problem
- encouraging use of the Emotional Toolbox
- helping to temporarily distract from angry, sad or anxious feelings and thoughts.

Ordinarily, social interactions can be stressful for young children with ASD, so it is important to choose these support people wisely. Choose people who:

- have genuine affection towards your child
- understand your child's strengths and difficulties
- listen to your child
- are patient with your child
- give emotional and practical support
- are not critical of your child
- do not shout.

Pets and animals can also be great to spend time with. Animals are often a great source of happiness and relaxation for people on the spectrum.

Introducing Social Tools

On page 92 of the Love and Affection Activity Booklet, there is a story in which Loving Lulu the Lemon explains that when she is worried or sad, she needs to use her Social Tools to help her to feel better. She explains what her Social Tools are, and who she enjoys spending time with. Her Social Tools include sharing time with people she likes and loves, asking for help and telling a friend or a grown-up how she feels. These are the three Social Tools, as described above.

On the next page in the Love and Affection Activity Booklet, there are suggestions for people with whom your child could use her Social Tools, and spaces to write down their names – for example, Mummy, Poppa. Below, there is an activity to complete to prepare for this discussion with your child.

Finally, the three Social Tools are described, and there is space to write down how these tools could be used.

Sometimes it can be difficult for a child with ASD to understand the value of using Social Tools. It is very helpful to have regular conversations with your child about the benefits of having people and animals that she likes and loves in her life. Whether the people who love us listen and offer validation, guidance and encouragement, laugh with us, enjoy an interest with us, express their affection for us, or are simply relaxing to spend time with us, these interactions can be the repair strategies we need when we are facing difficult emotions. For this reason, we include interactions with the people and animals we like and love in the Emotional Toolbox as Social Tools.

Description of the Activities

To begin the activity, read through the story, using the Loving Lulu the Lemon puppet to act it out. Have Loving Lulu the Lemon ask your child who helps him to feel better when he is worried, sad or angry, and compare who helps your child to feel better with who helps Loving Lulu the Lemon to feel better. Also, have Loving Lulu the Lemon ask your child how he asks for help and how often he asks for help. Then, on the next page, help your child to identify people he could go to for help and to feel better. Turn to page 94 and discuss the three Social Tools that your child could use to help him to feel better.

Finally, on the very last page of the Love and Affection Activity Booklet, there is a special message to your child from all the Feeling Friends in the form of a secret. Read this out to your child. If he has any questions, this special secret is a special message to your child to help him to remember that if one feeling is too strong, it can be very helpful to invite into his body the opposite of that feeling. For example, if your child is feeling sad, ask him to welcome in Happy Henry. He can use Happy Tools to do this. When he is anxious, ask him to invite Relaxed Ryan in by using Relaxation Tools. When Angry Alan visits, ask him to invite Loving Lulu to help, by thinking of the people who care about him, and which Social Tool he can use. Of course, any of the Tools in the Emotional Toolbox can be used for any of the emotions, but we have found that inviting the opposite feeling can be especially helpful.

Activity: People Who Love or Like My Child Who Could Help Her to Feel Better

It is helpful to think of some people to include as your child's 'go to' people for her to use her Social Tools with. Below is a list of potential Social Tools for young children with ASD. Read through the list and write the names of any people who would make good Social Tools for your child. Remember, the people to include are not only the people your child would go to if she was upset or worried, but also the people and animals that she simply enjoys spending time with or with whom she has interests in common.

- ☐ Family members: _____
- ☐ Adult family friend: _____
- ☐ Child family friend: _____
- ☐ Teacher: _____
- ☐ Other: _____
- ☐ Pets: _____

Practising Social Tools

As we have described, practising Social Tools involves spending time with the people and pets that your child enjoys, learning to ask for help when help is needed, and telling people who care about us how we are feeling. As with all earlier weeks, you will be scheduling into your Weekly Plan each of these activities. Both asking for help from another person and telling others how we feel involve skill and practice. We suggest that your child practises these skills a few times in the coming week.

When your child first practises asking for help, do so at a time when he is happy. It may be too overwhelming for your child to learn to ask for help while feeling anxious or angry. The first couple of practices should be role plays in which you, your child and the chosen support person role-play your child asking for help and then receiving help. Once your child understands how to ask for help and can use the skill when he is relaxed, encourage him to practise using this Social Tool when he is a little anxious, angry or sad.

Using Social Tools Yourself

As always, it is important that you practise using Social Tools yourself so that you can:

- ✓ have lower overall levels of stress, anxiety and depression
- ✓ more easily and confidently teach your child how to use Social Tools
- ✓ model effective emotion regulation to your child.

As for your child, you will benefit from having a range of people you can see for different reasons, including just being together because you enjoy that person's company. Take a moment now to note down who your key people are, whether you see these people enough, or whether you need more time with them, or even more support people in your life.

☐ Family members: _____
☐ Friends: _____
☐ Partner: _____
☐ Professional: _____
☐ Other: _____
☐ Pets: _____

Modelling Using Social Tools to Your Child

It is also important to model effective emotion regulation to your child by modelling effective use of the Social Tools of asking for help, spending time with people you love or like, and being able to recognize and label your own feelings. When you are anxious or stressed, show how to use Social Tools, perhaps using the following script:

> I just noticed that I am beginning to feel worried. My heart is beating faster and I feel sick in the tummy. I am going use a Social Tool and talk to my friend on the telephone. Feeling cared for by her always helps me feel calmer.

After speaking with your friend, share with your child how it helped:

> Aaah. I feel much calmer. Now I feel strong and I can cope even better.

As with previous tools, remember to adjust this script to suit your style and your child's level of understanding.

Encouraging Your Child to Use
Social Tools to Reduce Anxiety

When your child is comfortable using Social Tools and you have a list of people who will be supportive for your child in different situations, encourage your child to ask for help from these people. Regularly schedule in time that your child can spend with people she loves and/or likes.

To encourage your child to use the Social Tool of telling someone who cares about her how she is feeling, start with the more comfortable emotions of happy, relaxed and liking. Notice when your child is feeling one of these emotions. Say to your child, 'You look happy. Are you feeling happy?' If she agrees, affirm her by saying 'Great!' or even 'That makes me happy too!' If she disagrees, it is not important to prove you are right. Just shrug and say 'OK'.

Next, start to label the more uncomfortable emotions when you recognize them in your child. For example, you may say, 'You look a little angry. Are you feeling a little angry?' Remember that it is common for children with ASD to struggle to recognize and label their own emotions. This is a very important life skill that can take a child with ASD a long time to learn. Be prepared to be told that you are wrong. If this happens, just shrug and say 'OK'. You may be wrong. Children with ASD can be very difficult to read. If you are right, your child may not be able to admit that at the time, but your attempt to understand and validate her feelings is a very loving act and an extremely important part of building her understanding of feelings.

Weekly Plan Stage 10

The first goal for this week's Weekly Plan is to start teaching your child about affection, including the various levels of affection he experiences, how to identify liking and loving faces, and identifying what he feels in his body when he feels liking or loving toward someone. The second goal for the Weekly Plan is to start teaching your child how to use Social Tools. The third goal for this Weekly Plan is to practise another step from your child's Exposure Ladder.

Your Weekly Plan involves preparing for, scheduling and then completing the following activities with your child:

1. Meeting Loving Lulu the Lemon
2. Exploring different levels of affection with the Like/Love Thermometer
3. Mr Face
4. Like and Love Body Signs
5. Social Tools
6. Regular practice of Social Tools

7.   Modelling use of Social Tools
8.   Practising the Exposure Ladder step.

Action

Using the Weekly Plan, pencil in times that may be good times to schedule the five 2–10-minute activities with your child this week (Activities 1–5). Then, over the next week, at these scheduled times, complete each of the activities in the Love and Affection Activity Booklet with your child.

Once you have completed the Love and Affection Activity Booklet, schedule 2–10 minutes each day to practise the Social Tool of asking for help with your child when she is already calm and/or happy. Also, schedule in a time during the week for your child to spend one-on-one time with a person she enjoys being with – for example, you, another parent, grandparent or friend. Use the self-monitoring sheet to track progress and make any notes.

Throughout the week, try to notice times when you or your child are feeling affectionate. When you feel love or liking for a person or animal, share this experience with your child. If your child appears to be experiencing affection for a person or animal, ask her to share what she is feeling, like or love, the intensity on the Like/Love Thermometer, and where she can feel this emotion in her body.

Throughout the week also show your child how you cope with difficult emotions such as anger or worry using Social Tools.

Using the Weekly Plan, pencil in a time that may be a good time to practise a step on your child's Exposure Ladder. While completing the step, encourage your child to use the Emotional Tools she has already mastered – for example, Thought Tools, Relaxation Tools and Physical Tools.

Frequently Asked Questions

What if my child becomes more agitated by using the Social Tool of spending time with someone she likes?
It is difficult when, with all the good will in the world to assist your child to feel calmer and happier, you have scheduled a special time for them to be with a special person and the event triggers a meltdown, or your child seems more agitated after the special time than before. If this happens, do not despair. Part

of your child's ASD is that social time is one of their challenges, so time that can sometimes be replenishing at other times is draining and difficult for them. For next time, consider whether background stress factors were managed (your child was well rested and fed and not thirsty, and that the sensory environment was not too challenging), consider shortening the duration of the contact, and consider a different person or a different setting.

Activity: Anxiety Survival Plan

In Stage 2 we introduced your Anxiety Survival Plan, which is in Appendix A. The Anxiety Survival Plan was included to become a quick guide for anyone who is involved in your child's care to use to effectively identify and manage your child's anxiety, based on all you have learned about your child, and what helps to decrease her anxiety, during the *Fun with Feelings* programme. As described earlier, on this Survival Plan is a thermometer with room for you to write your child's anxiety triggers and signs (behaviours), as well as helpful strategies for reducing anxiety when your child is experiencing small, medium and large levels of anxiety. Now that you have completed the programme, you have earned a wealth of knowledge about the triggers for anxiety for your child, their signs of anxiety and strategies for managing each level of anxiety. Take some time now to add this knowledge to your Anxiety Survival Plan. This will be invaluable knowledge for home, school and therapy settings.

Top Tip

A child may experience a high level of anxiety and still be able to employ a strategy to cope – for example, jumping on the trampoline to burn off the physical tension. However, when they go into meltdown, remember that they are overwhelmed and the thinking part of their brain is closed, and we need to use a different strategy to assist the thinking part of their brain to come 'online' again – for example, decreasing stimulation to the brain by removing people or by seeking quiet or solitude.

Social Tools Practice Monitoring Form

Day	Social Tool practised (e.g. asking for help or spending time with someone)	Comments
1		
2		
3		
4		
5		
6		
7		

Final Word

Congratulations! You have now completed the *Fun with Feelings* programme. We hope that you have enjoyed the programme, including learning about anxiety with your child, as well as the five other basic emotions. It is our fervent hope that you feel empowered as a result of the time you have spent absorbing new knowledge and implementing the new strategies. We hope that the information has been validating and useful.

Anxiety is a condition that comes and goes throughout a person's life. Research shows that, for children with ASD, anxiety increases during primary school, and again in high school (Mayes *et al.*, 2011). What you have achieved by following this programme, learning your child's triggers and signs of anxiety, as well as the strategies that help, sets in place one of the best possible foundations you can give your child for his life. Over time, many of these signs, triggers and strategies will change. Continuing to assist your child to know his own triggers and signs, and to learn the strategies that work, will prepare him to face the challenges ahead.

We encourage you to look after yourself in these ways, as much as you do for your child or children, and to treat yourself with the same love and compassion. You are one of the most important resources your child has. By managing your own anxiety and treating yourself with love and compassion, you are not only ensuring you have the energy to be there for your child – you are also teaching him how to live.

We wish you all the best on this amazing journey!

Michelle, Tony, Louise, Stef and Julia

Appendix A: Anxiety Survival Plan

First, complete the table on the next page. When you have completed the table, add any information from it that will be useful to an adult to assist your child to manage their anxiety, at low, medium and high levels. When adults know the triggers, signs of anxiety and what helps, for each level of anxiety, they will be much better equipped to assist your child.

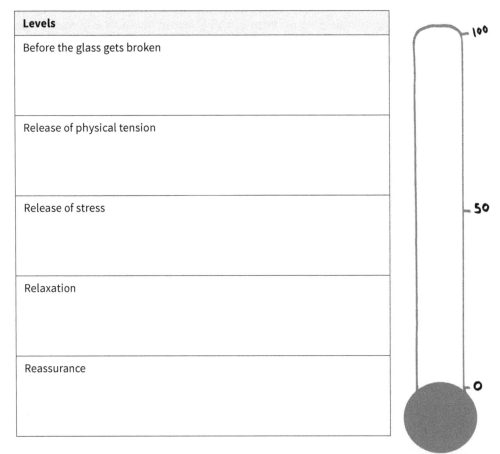

Levels
Before the glass gets broken
Release of physical tension
Release of stress
Relaxation
Reassurance

Triggers of big anxiety	Signs of big anxiety	Strategies for big anxiety

Triggers of medium anxiety	Signs of medium anxiety	Strategies for medium anxiety

Triggers of small anxiety	Signs of small anxiety	Strategies for small anxiety

Appendix B: Instructions to Prepare the Puppets for the Programme

Using scissors, cut out each fruit character and the rectangle the appears next to each character. Next, using Sellotape, secure each end of the rectangle onto the back of each fruit, such that a loop is formed. The fruit becomes a puppet when you insert your finger through the loop. You may ask your child to colour in each puppet before using them.

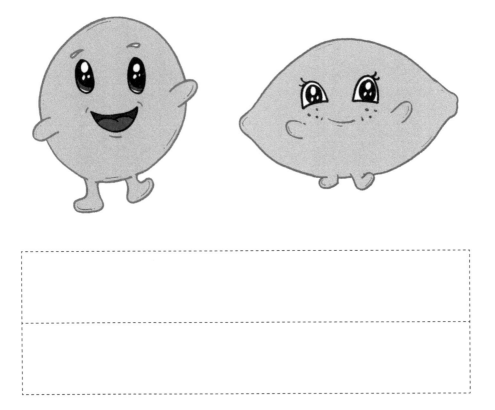

References

American Psychiatric Association (2013) *Diagnostic and Statistical Manual of Mental Disorders, 5th Edition*. Washington, DC: American Psychiatric Association.

Attwood, T. (2004) *Exploring Feelings: Cognitive Behaviour Therapy to Manage Anxiety*. Arlington, TX: Future Horizons.

Attwood, T. (2006) *The Complete Guide to Asperger's Syndrome*. Jessica Kingsley Publishers: London.

Attwood, T. and Garnett, M. (2013a) *From Like to Love for Young People with Asperger's Syndrome (Autism Spectrum Disorder): Learning How to Express and Enjoy Affection with Family and Friends*. London: Jessica Kingsley Publishers.

Attwood, T. and Garnett, M. (2013b) *From Like to Love within Friendships and Family: Cognitive Behaviour Therapy to Understand and Express Affection*. London: Jessica Kingsley Publishers.

Baio, J., Wiggins, L., Christensen, D.L., Maenner, M.J. *et al.* (2018) 'Prevalence of autism spectrum disorder among children aged 8 years – Autism and Developmental Disabilities Monitoring Network, 11 sites, United States, 2014.' *MMWR Surveillance Summaries* 67, SS-6, 1–23.

Clarke, C., Hill, V. and Charman, T. (2017) 'School based cognitive behavioural therapy targeting anxiety in children with autistic spectrum disorder: A quasi-experimental randomised controlled trial incorporating a mixed methods approach.' *Journal of Autism and Developmental Disorders* 47, 12, 3883–3895.

Cook, J.M., Donovan, C.L. and Garnett, M.S. (2017) 'A parent-mediated, cognitive behavioral therapy group treatment for young children with high-functioning autism spectrum disorder and comorbid anxiety: Development and case illustration of the Fun with Feelings program.' *Journal of Cognitive Psychotherapy* 31, 3, 204–224.

Doran, G.T. (1981) 'There's a S.M.A.R.T. way to write management's goals and objectives.' *Management Review* 70, 11, 35–36.

Ecker, C. (2017) 'The neuroanatomy of autism spectrum disorder: An overview of structural neuroimaging findings and their translatability to the clinical setting.' *Autism* 21, 1, 18–28.

Gray, C. (2010) *The New Social Story™ Book*. Arlington, TX: Future Horizons.

Gray, C. (2015) *The New Social Story Book*. Future Horizons: US.

Lever, A.G. and Geurts, H.M. (2016) 'Psychiatric co-occurring symptoms and disorders in young, middle-aged, and older adults with autism spectrum disorder.' *Journal of Autism and Developmental Disorders 46*, 6, 1916–1930.

Luxford, S., Hadwin, J.A. and Kovshoff, H. (2017) 'Evaluating the effectiveness of a school-based cognitive behavioural therapy intervention for anxiety in adolescents diagnosed with autism spectrum disorder.' *Journal of Autism and Developmental Disorders 47*, 12, 3896–3908.

Mayes, S.D., Calhoun, S.L., Murray, M.J. and Zahid, J. (2011) 'Variables associated with anxiety and depression in children with autism.' *Journal of Developmental and Physical Disabilities 23*, 4, 325–337.

McConachie, H., McLaughlin, E., Grahame, V., Taylor, H. *et al.* (2014) 'Group therapy for anxiety in children with autism spectrum disorder.' *Autism 18*, 6, 723–732.

Plows, S. (2013) 'Fun with Feelings: An Emotion Management Program for 4–6-year-old Children with Asperger's Syndrome.' Unpublished doctoral dissertation, Griffith University, Brisbane, Queensland, Australia.

Russell, E. and Sofronoff, K. (2005) 'Anxiety and social worries in children with Asperger syndrome.' *Australian and New Zealand Journal of Psychiatry 39*, 7, 633–638.

Rutherford, M., McKenzie, K., Johnson, T., Catchpole, C. *et al.* (2016) 'Gender ratio in a clinical population sample, age of diagnosis and duration of assessment in children and adults with autism spectrum disorder.' *Autism 20*, 5, 628–634.

Sofronoff, K., Attwood, T. and Hinton, S. (2005) 'A randomised controlled trial of a CBT intervention for anxiety in children with Asperger syndrome.' *Journal of Child Psychology and Psychiatry 46*, 11, 1152–1160.

Sofronoff, K., Attwood, T., Hinton, S. and Levin, I. (2007) 'A randomized controlled trial of a cognitive behavioural intervention for anger management in children diagnosed with Asperger syndrome.' *Journal of Autism and Developmental Disorders 37*, 7, 1203–1214.

Strang, J.F., Kenworthy, L., Daniolos, P., Case, L. *et al.* (2012) 'Depression and anxiety symptoms in children and adolescents with autism spectrum disorders without intellectual disability.' *Research in Autism Spectrum Disorders 6*, 1, 406–412.

Timmins, S. (2016) *Successful Social Stories™ for Young Children with Autism: Growing Up with Social Stories™*. London: Jessica Kingsley Publishers.